Dedicated to You Drivers

**The next time you're caught
in the web of one of these.**

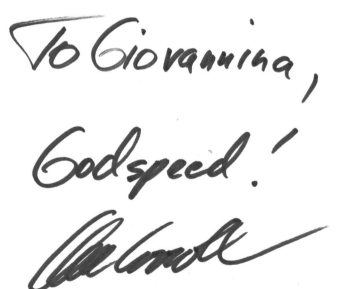

To Giovannina,

Godspeed!

To Giovanino(?)

Godspeed!

Speeding Excuses That Work

The Cleverest Copouts & Ticket Victories Ever!

By Alex Carroll

Illustrated by
Joe Azar

gray area press

Gray Area Press
924 Chapala Street, Suite D, Santa Barbara, CA 93101

Library of Congress Catalog Number: 2001097201
ISBN: 0-9634641-3-2

Book packaging by CorkScrew Press

Cover design by Ken Niles

Single-copy orders: (866) COPOUTS [866-267-6887]

Quantity Orders: (805) 564-6868

Book Trade: Contact Ingram Book Group or Baker & Taylor

For free updates and new ticket stories, visit **copouts.com**

Printed in the United States of America

This book contains true
stories from drivers who
outfoxed the cops and
escaped traffic tickets.

Now their secrets can
work for you, too.

Disclaimer

This book contains information based on current U.S. and state laws, as well as personal experiences related to the publisher from the general public via email. While the information in this book is believed to be accurate, neither the author nor the publisher is engaged in rendering legal, medical or other professional advice, and is not responsible for any loss or damage resulting from reliance on the contents of this book. The names have been genetically modified to protect the guilty.

Contents

The Excuses • 19-56

Page 140

Bonus Section

More Excuses • 103-154

Page 145

Does This Book Encourage You...

...To Break The Law?

Maybe...maybe not. Depends on what the speed limit is, and what the law says.

Common sense will tell you that the safest speed is *with* the flow...no matter what the sign says.

I'm encouraging you to go with the flow. If that happens to be against the law, then you have a decision to make. You can obey the laws of misguided legislators, or you can obey the laws of physics. Personally, I'm always going to choose a safe speed over a "legal" one.

As for those of you who whine that my "encouraging people to break the law" fosters a general disregard for law and order...you really need a reality check.

Consider this: Did you know that as I write this, it's against the law to fly a kite in Chicago? Did you know it's also illegal to talk on an elevator in New York, sing in the bathtub in Pennsylvania, and sleep naked in Minnesota? And get this...it is a violation for a woman to wear pants in Tucson!

The point is this. There are thousands of ridiculous laws on the books. Just because it's written in law, does not necessarily mean it's written in stone.

I wonder how many of you 'law-abiding citizens' would reconsider your position if you got dinged for a few minor vehicle infractions. Any cop will tell you that all he has to do is follow ANYONE for a block or two and they will have broken at least one traffic law.

Look, this book is not for morons who scream through school zones or treat neighborhood streets like raceways. It's for normal drivers caught up in outdated laws, overzealous cops, speed traps designed to enrich local governments, and dozens of situations where safety is compromised by foolhardy rigidity.

My advice to you is to keep your eyes on the road, stay alert and go with the flow. And if you do get stopped, well...that's why you bought this book.

Memo To All Cops

Look, I realize this book is full of lies—and I realize you're the ones being lied to. And I know you may have a real problem with that. Fair enough.

But I ask you, which came first: the speed trap— or the excuse? A speed trap is inherently dishonest. And dishonesty breeds more dishonesty. Fighting fire with fire is an instinctual reaction. I'm not saying two wrongs make a right—I'm just pointing out the inevitable dynamics of the situation. Think about it.

I appeal to each of you: be agents of traffic safety —not agents of traffic revenue. Go after the reckless drivers, the impaired drivers, the inattentive drivers yapping on cell phones. They are the real dangers on the road today. Try to give up the practice of setting up speed traps just to fill some real or imagined quota at the expense of easy-to-catch motorists who really aren't endangering anyone. If they're going with the flow—leave 'em alone. If they don't quite come to a complete stop at a deserted intersection—let 'em be.

And for heaven's sake, don't write people double-fine construction-zone speeding tickets on Sunday evening when there's not a hardhat in sight. Have a heart. Be fair. Tickets and insurance surcharges are a pricey proposition these days. Do these people really deserve this kind of punishment?

Think "spirit" of the law vs. "letter" of the law. As Sergeant Drinkwater tells his guys, "The only thing black and white about this job is the car you drive."

I know the vast majority of cops today are good. You take pride in your work and uphold the honor of the badge. You know who you are. Many of you are personal friends. I know you'll enjoy the candor and humor of this book—and I'm sure more than a few copies will find their way into the donut shop.

But there's a minority of cops who DO NOT belong in law enforcement—or any other job that involves human contact. You know who you are. You don't catch criminals—you ARE criminals. I've met a few of you—you're a disgrace to the badge, and humanity.

If you're brass—and you've got one of these guys working for you—do us all a favor and get rid of him.

Memo to the good cops...

Thank you for all you do. I appreciate each of you for making this country one of the safest places in the world. When I travel, I realize how lucky we are. I know you put your lives on the line every day. I know about the AIDS-infested street urchins who scratch, bite and blow chunks in the back of your cruiser. I know about the emergency calls in the middle of the night. I know about the morons and perps you face every day. I know what you deal with—and you have my unwavering respect and deepest gratitude.

Subject: **Pop-Eye**
Date: Fri, 30 Mar
From: PενεσσM<PενεεM@γτε.net >
To: copouts@copouts.com

I was driving along, minding my own business, when I glanced up and saw that spinning red light. Before the cop could reach my door, I pulled one of my disposable contact lenses out of my eye.

"Did you know you were doing 25 miles over the speed limit?" the officer asked.

"Yes," I said. "My contact fell out of my eye, and I am just hurrying to find a place to stop and place it back in." The cop told me he had never heard such a story before, and he let me go. I am telling you this works every time! Just carry a disposable contact lens in your car that is available when the need arises.

Subject: **Catch A Wave**
Date: Thurs, 26 April
From: Δ Ηαμιλτον <ηαμιλτον22@ηομε.com >
To: copouts@copouts.com

My brother-in-law is a Cincinnati cop who told me he'd never pull someone over who waved at him, because that person is probably a cop, too. So...I'm driving back from Cincy doin' about 85 mph, when I see Mr. State Patrol on the median, beaming my way. His head jerks up as his radar screams, and as I fly past, I smile and wave. And guess what? HE WAVED BACK and did not pursue me!

Overheard At The Donut Shop

A policeman staked out his favorite spot to watch for speeders, but wasn't getting any that day. Then he discovered why: a ten-year-old boy was standing further up the road with a hand-painted sign that read, "SPEED TRAP AHEAD."

The officer then found a young accomplice down the road with another hand-painted sign that read, "TIPS"—together with a bucketful of change.

Subject: Preemptive Strike

Date: Mon, 28 May

From: ΜΣχηοφιελδ<σχοφιελδ@αολ.com >

To: copouts@copouts.com

While cutting through a small Kansas town to shorten my drive from one major turnpike to another, I was doing about 45 mph in a 30 zone. Suddenly I spotted a radar officer parked in a church driveway, pointing his radar gun at me. Since I knew I was going to be stopped anyway, I pulled a tight turn directly into the church driveway, rolled down my window and said, "I'm so glad I found you! I'm hopelessly lost—can you tell me how to get to the turnpike?" He was so stunned at my actions, he gave me directions and even offered to have me follow him to the turnpike!

Editor's Note: *A map in your lap would make this even more effective.*

Subject: **Unemployment Card**
Date: Wed, 11 April
From: M.Νοτο<μνοτο@ηομε.com >
To: copouts@copouts.com

For two bucks, I get out of speeding tickets. I simply keep a large mushy *We're Gonna Miss You* greeting card inside my glove box, signed by 20 or 30 former co-workers. Of course, I simply use different colored pens to scribble a whole bunch of fake names inside. When pulled over, I explain to the officer that I'm sorry if I was speeding, but I'm too overcome with despair for being the latest victim of corporate downsizing, because I just left my job of ten years for the last time and yada yada yada. Then I hang my head, show him the card, and play on his sympathy for my dire economic situation.

Subject: **Hose Job**

Date: Thurs, 19 July
From: ΡαχερΞΜΝΩ <Ραχερ354@αολ.com >
To: copouts@copouts.com

I was travelling at a higher rate of speed than usual in an empty industrial section of town at 6 a.m. one Saturday morning, when I rounded a hard corner and proceeded onto the highway in a hurry. At that corner is the Sheriff's Office—and they must have spotted me from the parking lot. When the officer eventually caught up, he appeared a little nervous, probably fearing I had just burglarized a business, so I knew this would be a hard sell.

I explained that my waterbed had sprung a leak, and water was leaking all over the floor of my third-story apartment. Pointing to the garden hose I'd just retrieved from work, I explained there was no place to purchase a hose in town at 6 a.m. While he was scratching his head, I offered to let him follow me home if he didn't believe me, but he would have to issue the ticket after we got there, because I was leaving! He just told me to slow down, and I pulled off in a blaze. Since that incident, I now carry a hose in my car all the time!

Subject: **Sucker!**

Date: Thurs, 6 Sept

From: ☐Βιγ Τ<Βτγτμυρδερ@εξχιτε.com >

To: copouts@copouts.com

I was doing 85 mph in a 65 zone when the state trooper caught me in his radar. As he swaggered toward my car, I pulled the suckie from my two-year-old's mouth, knowing exactly what would happen. When I  opened the window, I couldn't even hear the trooper's questions over the screaming. I yelled that I was not aware of my speed because I was just about to pull over at the next rest stop till he calmed down. To top it off, my kid's crying got even louder. After checking my license and registration, he let me go with just a warning.

Subject: **Bug Off!**
Date: Fri, 11 May
From: ΑλεξΓ <ςενεζυλα@ηομε.com >
To: copouts@copouts.com

I was driving solo on I-5 through Washington State, bored to death, when suddenly this big ugly black bug *thwaps* right onto my windshield. After about three miles of watching it hold on for dear life, I started wondering how much wind it would take to knock that critter off my glass (with no help from the squirter or wipers). So I start accelerating—all the way up to 92 mph. I was so focused on the bug in the front, I didn't notice the state trooper in the rear.

After he pulls me over and asks what I was doing, I figured I'd try to explain my science experiment. Luckily, the test subject was still clinging to my windshield. That trooper laughed so hard, he just gave me a warning, and told me it was the best excuse he'd ever heard.

But there's more. He must have called a radio station later that day, because I heard the local DJs cracking up about the bug's good fortune—and mine.

Subject: Short Circuit
Date: Sat, 10 Feb
From: □Ωιλλψβοψ <φοτοβιλλ@αολ.com >
To: copouts@copouts.com

The advanced technology on my new car gave me a ticket-avoiding idea I finally got to try the other day. As Officer Friendly was looking for an acceptable place to U-turn after spotting me speeding, it was all the time I needed to locate the fuse box to pull the fuse to my digital dashboard. When he asked if I knew why I was pulled over, I said in my most polite and naïve tone that it was probably for excessive speed, but I couldn't be sure because the fuse to my digital dash had just blown and my instruments weren't working. I explained that even though I'd been trying to gauge what 55 feels like, there were no other cars on the road to pace. He huffed I'd been going 75. I politely replied I was incredibly sorry for the inconvenience, and the dealer is expecting the new fuse to arrive that afternoon so this wouldn't happen again. He let me go with a warning.

Subject: Here Spike!

Date: Sat, 14 May

From: ☐Ωιλλψβοψ <φοτοβιλλ@αολ.com>

To: copouts@copouts.com

Keep a spare dog leash and choker collar in your car. The next time you get pulled over, tell the cop your friend is on vacation, you are watching his pit bull for him, and you just got a call that "Spike" got out of the yard and is running loose in the neighborhood and you're going to look for him. This works best if your "friend's" house is outside the cop's jurisdiction, but if he offers to help track down the dog, the worst that could happen is the damn dog has disappeared!

Overheard At The Donut Shop

A man who was in no shape to drive, wisely decided to leave his car parked and walk home. As he was walking unsteadily along, he was stopped by a cop.

"What are you doing out here at 2 am?" he asked.

"I'm going to a lecture," said the man.

"And WHO is giving a lecture at THIS hour?" the cop demanded.

"My wife," said the man.

Subject: **Shake Down**
Date: Thurs, 26 July
From: Αχεγυε <αχεγιψ976@αολ.com >
To: copouts@copouts.com

My Auntie has epilepsy. A couple of years ago, Mum sent me down to the drugstore to pick up her medication. On the way back, I must have been going a little over the speed limit because a policeman stopped me. When he asked me what was the hurry, I showed him the bottle and explained that I needed to get these to my Auntie right away. He just said okay and told me to slow it down a little. Well, I asked my Auntie if I could have that bottle when she was finished with it. She said sure. When she gave it to me, I filled it with aspirin and put it in my car. It's already saved me a couple more times.

> **Editor's Note:** Anyone with a bottle for any unpronounceable prescription could use this one. How is a cop going to know whether it's for epilepsy or not?

I'd just bought your last book, *Beat The Cops*, to help me fight a ticket. But when I got pulled over AGAIN, I noticed on the seat next to me—in plain sight—was my subpoena, my speeding ticket...and *your book* (with that picture of the big fat cop on the front).

I quickly and nonchalantly tossed the nearest sheet of paper on top to hide them. As the younger officer came up to my window and started grilling me, his partner stood silently on the passenger side. This was really not my day, because in addition to having just lost my driver's license card, I was horrified to observe that the sheet of paper I'd used to cover everything was my proof of insurance. So when I handed over all the paperwork, the other cop instantly spotted your book. "Hey, what's THAT?" he demanded. I admitted I was fighting another ticket. "Let's see the book," he said. I braced for the worst. But then, they just burst out laughing! They took my license number off my previous ticket and ran it back at their cruiser. When they returned to my car, they were still cracking up! Then off they drove, without *ever* telling me what they pulled me over for!

A woman friend from college had just broken up with her boyfriend. She was upset, angry, crying—and driving over 50 mph in a 35 zone, when she was pulled over by a young policeman.

She was hunched over the wheel as he walked up to her car. "What's wrong?" he asked, observing her tear-streaked face. "I'm bleeding! I think I'm miscarrying," she moaned. "The emergency room doctor said to get there as fast as I can." He apologized for stopping her and made sure she knew how to get to the hospital.

> **Editor's Note:** Don't try this if you're obviously over 50.

Subject: **Oil's Well**
Date: Thurs, 19 April
From: ΜιχηελεΩ <Μιχηελλε@αολ.com>
To: copouts@copouts.com

About a week ago, I was speeding through town when a cop saw me, flipped on his cherries, and attempted to pull me over. I was in the middle of town, so I sped up as he followed, racing to the nearest gas station to stop my vehicle. Before the cop came to my door, I frantically jumped out of my vehicle and popped my hood. The cop asked me what I was doing, speeding and eluding a police officer? I explained with great emotion that my oil light had just come on, and I thought my engine was going to blow up, so I was racing to the nearest gas station. It must have been a convincing story, because he helped me check my oil before going on his way. *WHEW!*

Subject: **Double Dribble**
Date: Fri, 11 May
From: ΚρισΡ <ΚρισΡοβο@ηομε.com >
To: copouts@copouts.com

I was speeding to work one day when I got pulled over by a cop. He asked me if I knew how fast I was going, and I told him I had good reason for going that speed. Now before I tell you how I totally got out of that speeding ticket, you should know I'm young, blonde and built.

Anyway, the cop asked me what my 'good reason' was, and I told him that a few minutes earlier, I'd fallen down the stairs and was afraid that one of my breast implants had sprung a leak. After his eyes returned from my chest, I heaped it on by looking like I was about to cry. I told him I was rushing to the hospital to get it checked out, and that did the trick— he let me go right away. But the funny thing is, I don't have implants!

Subject: **Wrong Number**
Date: Fri, 9 Feb
From: ☐Αννα Κεψ <αννακεψ@ηομε.com>
To: copouts@copouts.com

When visiting from England, my brother got himself utterly turned around on the freeway. After driving lost for 30 minutes—at speeds between 80 and 100 mph—he was pulled over by the Highway Patrol. Over the loudspeaker, the cops blared, "Take the key out of the ignition, and get out with your hands in the air." The cops frisked him, and asked for all the documents. Hearing his accent, they asked how long he'd been in the country, and why he was going so fast. Didn't he know there was a speed limit?

"A speed limit with the roads so wide—why would you need one?" he replied. The cops pointed to the 50 mph sign. "Oh... I thought that was the HIGHWAY number!" he said. They gave him a verbal warning, drew him a map and were just about to pull away when he flagged them down and asked for a bump start, as he had flooded the engine. When he told us this story, he said it was just like in the movies.

Date: Wed, 25 April
From: M.Νοτο<μνοτο@ηομε.com >
To: copouts@copouts.com

What a day I'd had. I was driving back from the doctor after an embarrassing treatment for genital warts. When the cop pulled me over for speeding, I told him I was rushing to the drugstore to get the prescription ointment to cool the burning where they'd removed the warts.

I showed him the treatment information brochure and tried to hand it to him as I winced in pain. He looked at me like I had the plague or something, and couldn't send me on my way fast enough. Needless to say, I now keep that brochure in the car all the time. It hasn't failed me yet.

> **Editor's Note:** Be sure to stash that brochure if you're on a date.

Subject: **Uniformity**
Date: Mon, 4 Sept
From: ☐Μαρκ Σ.<μαρκσ@ηυμ.net >
To: copouts@copouts.com

I once dated a girl who worked in a nursing home. While driving her to work one night, we were pulled over for speeding. As luck would have it, she had her uniform on a hanger in the back of my car. I told the officer that she had been called in early for an emergency. Worked like a charm!

Overheard At The Donut Shop

While driving cross-country, an elderly couple gets pulled over by a cop. "Ma'am, did you know you were speeding?" asks the officer. She turns to her husband and asks, "What'd he say?" The old man yells, "HE SAYS YOU WERE SPEEDING."

"May I see your license?" asks the cop. She again turns to her husband and asks, "What'd he say?" The old man yells, "HE WANTS TO SEE YOUR LICENSE."

While looking at the license, the cop remarks, "I see you're from Arkansas. Once when I was there, I had the worst sex with a woman I've *ever* had." The woman turns to her husband and asks, "What'd he say?" The old man yells, "HE THINKS HE KNOWS YOU."

Subject: **Break A Leg**
Date: Thurs, 26 July
From: ☐ΧρανκΒαιτ <χρανκβαιτ@ψαηοο.com >
To: copouts@copouts.com

As anyone will tell you, a mother's car is easy to identify: well-worn car seat, empty juice boxes, crayons, toys and general goo. So when I got pulled over for speeding to a nail appointment, my messy car became the perfect set for my instant mini-drama.

I looked that cop straight in the eye and poured on an Academy Award-winning performance: "I just got a call from the babysitter. My daughter has gotten sicker and now she's THROWING UP!" Then, with panic creeping into my voice, I continued, "I'm on my way home from work to take her to the hospital. So if you're going to give me a ticket, PLEASE write it quickly so I can get home!" And you guessed it—I was on my way. I'd like to thank the Academy, my adorable daughter, our nonexistent babysitter, as well as that sweetheart of a cop!

Subject: Collared

Date: Thurs, 26 July

From: ☐Αχετησ <αχετησ@ψαηοο.com >

To: copouts@copouts.com

I'm a travelling salesman in the pharmaceutical industry. I used to get nailed all the time. Then I came up with a plan. I bought one of those Roman collars (like the ones that priests wear) and a couple of black shirts. I also got one of those, "God is my co-pilot" bumper stickers. Now when I hit the road, I always don my "uniform." I don't know what it is about priests, but cops just don't bother me anymore. I'm sure it won't help me out much when I get to the pearly gates, but it sure has cleaned up my driving record.

Editor's Note: A bible in your backseat might make this even more convincing.

Subject: **Phantom Flirt**
Date: Sun, 11 Aug
From: □Παυλ Ρηοδεσ <Πρηοδεσ@αολ.com >
To: copouts@copouts.com

It was a beautiful spring day and I was driving my '65 Mustang down a 4-lane road, windows open, rockin' out. As I came to a stoplight turning yellow, I had a choice: quickly stop, or gun-n-run. I chose the latter.

I guess I wasn't paying attention, because there was a cop sitting in a gas station across the street. Of course, I was pulled over and took my ticket like a man. Having tried this once or twice before, I figured I had a better chance of fighting the ticket in court than arguing with the cop.

The court was in a relatively small town, and as such, there was just the cop, the judge, and me. It was pretty informal. I was asked how I wanted to plead. I said, "You know, your honor, I am probably guilty of running the red light, but I have to claim mitigating circumstances." He said, "How so?"

So, I took a chance and I created a story. I said, "Your honor, as the officer here will probably attest, it was a magnificent spring day when I was pulled over. Why do I remember that? Because, as I was driving down the street, I noticed a hot, red Camaro convertible

driving along side of me. The top was down and in the driver's seat was a gorgeous blonde, hair flying in the wind!"

"I was looking admiringly over at her and, when I looked back, I saw that the light was yellow. I was very close to the intersection, and had to make a decision. Should I try to make it through the yellow, or try to stop? I felt that it would be safer to run the yellow light."

"Of course, then the light turned red. The officer, rightly so, pulled me over. That's my story, and you can see why I might claim mitigating circumstances. I have to blame it on the fact that I was transfixed by the blonde driving next to me."

The judge looked at me, looked at the cop, and said with a smile, "This story seems to have a ring of truth to it. Although I cannot condone this type of activity, I'm inclined to let this young man off with a stern warning." And so it was.

I learned a valuable lesson. Whether you are quick on your feet and are able to conjure a story on the fly, or plan to attack the validity of the ticket, you always have a chance to beat it, if you go to court.

Subject: **Intestinal Fartitude**
Date: Sun, 18 Feb
From: Δογυστερ<Ρινγψ@ηομε.com >
To: copouts@copouts.com

Visit one of those gag-gift stores at the mall and pick up a bottle of fart-scented air freshener. When you hear the siren and see the lights, let 'er rip, stash the bottle out of sight—and leave your windows rolled up! When the officer reaches your door, roll down the window and tell him with the utmost urgency that you've got Crohn's disease and have to get to a toilet right away. Works for me everytime.

Editor's Note: *Crohn's ["crones"] is an intestinal disease that causes constant stomach pain and diarrhea.*

Subject: **No Control**
Date: Wed, 11 July
From: □Χαρεψ Χ <λαβρατσ@ψαηοο.com >
To: copouts@copouts.com

I was traveling south on I-75 in Michigan, coming from the Upper Peninsula, when a state trooper on an overpass clocked me going 90 mph in a 65. When he stopped me, he immediately asked if I knew how fast I was going. "Yes, around 90 mph," I replied. He appeared shocked at my honest admission, but I followed it up by saying the car I was driving was actually my passenger's, and I was trying to figure out the cruise control when the accelerator button got stuck, and I panicked because I didn't know what to do. At that, the officer let me go with warning. Little did he know the '91 Honda didn't even have cruise control on it!

Subject: **Surgical Strike**
Date: Fri, 24 Aug
From: Ροσσ Λ<σχομαν@ηομε.com >
To: copouts@copouts.com

My excuse has worked 3 times in 2 different states, and the best part is it's so easy to pull off.

When I get pulled over for speeding, I tell the officer I've got to pick up my sister because my father just fell off a ladder and he's about to go into surgery for a mangled leg. My mother called and said the doctor thinks he might not be able to save the leg unless my sister and I get to the hospital right away to give blood for the surgery.

You can modify this story any way you like, of course, as long as you appear very sincere in your delivery. Not only have I gotten off 3 times without a ticket, I always get best wishes from the officer!

I beat a ticket by saying all this in one breath, and I'll bet you can too:

I'm sorry if I was going too fast but a friend of my wife just called to say she was down at the pound looking for a dog to adopt and while they were looking she thought she saw our dog Boomer who ran away from us three weeks ago and we have had him since he was a puppy and our kids love him to death so my wife's friend asked about the dog and they told her that since no one claimed him and he hasn't been adopted they will be putting him to sleep today so my wife tried to call the pound to tell them the dog is ours and we will come down there to get him right away but the phone has been busy at the pound for the last 1 1/2 hours and she can't get through so she called me and told me to get to the pound ASAP to try to get Boomer before you-know-what happens and she didn't want to take the kids in case we got there too late and that is why I am in such a hurry!

Subject: **Brothers In Arms**
Date: Fri, 20 July
From: ☐ΡιχκΣ <ΦΦΠπαραμεδχ@ηομε.com>
To: copouts@copouts.com

Most people have heard about "professional courtesies" given by cops to members of other professional career fields who they may need to deal with in the future—especially firefighters and paramedics. I'd heard it working as a paramedic, but hadn't needed it for several years.

Well, I was driving home about 3 a.m. after a shift as a paramedic in Detroit. I was extremely tired, and apparently not paying much attention to what I was doing. I was pulled over for doing 70 mph through a zone where the speed limit dropped from 55 to 45.

While the cop was explaining why he pulled me over, he apparently saw the paramedic patch on my shoulder. I explained I'd just come off shift and probably should've taken a nap before leaving. He immediately apologized for pulling me over and told me to go get some sleep and left.

Ever since, I leave my paramedic jacket draped over the driver's seat as a notice to cops who pull me over—and although I've only been pulled over a couple times—I haven't received a ticket yet.

Subject: **Take THAT!**
Date: Tues, 7 May
From: ☐Κατηψ M<νιγητσβανε@ηομε.net>
To: copouts@copouts.com

A while back, I made the mistake of buying one of those cheapo radar detector things.

After already getting nailed twice, I got pulled over for a third time. I was not happy. So when the cop got to the window, I just ripped the damn thing right off the dashboard and said, "Here, YOU take it...piece of &%$#@ doesn't work anyway!"

He started chuckling and asked for my license and reg. He was still laughing when he came back from his car and told me to slow it down and have a nice day.

NO TICKET!!

Editor's Note: *This could really work quite well. Just buy a cheap detector and keep it in your car.*

Subject: Fake I.D.

Date: Fri, 4 May
From: ☐ ΣΗοψτ <σφηπατσφαν@ηομε.com >
To: copouts@copouts.com

I was cruising back from a Bruins game on I-93 and was nabbed on radar by a state trooper for going 20 mph over the speed limit. An attorney friend of mine offered to handle the case in exchange for lunch.

After continuing the case a couple of times, my lawyer, a friend of his and I appeared in court. When my case was called, and I sat quietly with my attorney's friend while the trooper went on for 15 minutes about how he had just calibrated the gun, how fast I was going, etc. When he finished, my lawyer said, "Your honor, I move this case be dismissed. The prosecutor has failed to identify the defendant." The judge looked over to the trooper and said, "Well, can you identify the defendant?" The trooper looked at the me, and then at my attorney's friend, and said, "I'm 99.9% sure it was the gentleman sitting with his arms folded, but I'm not going to risk my 20-year reputation over a speeding ticket. No your honor, I can't." With that, the judge dismissed the case. On our way out, the trooper asked my lawyer if he was right. I was more than happy to tell him he wasn't!

Subject: **False Positive**
Date: Mon, 5 March
From: Μικε Οβρινε <Μικεολ@τβιρδ.com >
To: copouts@copouts.com

I was 16 and going to pick up my girlfriend from work. It was about 11:30 pm and I was going 55 in a 45. When the cop pulled me over, I tried to look as dazed as possible without

breaking a smile. When he asked, "where's the big emergency," I started blubbering (whining, not crying) about just finding out my girlfriend was pregnant. I told him I was 16 and didn't know what I was going to do and I was scared to go home. Not only did I get out of the ticket, but he stayed with me for a good ten minutes until I could "calm down." Needless to say, I was pretty pleased with myself and had a funny story to share with my girl.

It was early November and I got stopped for speeding. My husband had already gotten a couple of tickets, so our insurance couldn't afford another one.

So I'm trying to think of something to say as I look around at the mess the kids left in the car, when I see these fake blood capsules on the console, left over from Halloween.

And then it hits me: NOSEBLEED!!

I know this sounds gross, but I grabbed one of the capsules and kinda squished it up my nose. When the cop saw all the blood dripping from my nose, he apologized for stopping me and told me to hurry on home. I told him that's exactly what I was doing.

I'm just glad my kids weren't with me. They probably would've been laughing so much I'm sure it would've spoiled it.

Speeding Excuse Cheat Sheet

Tear this out. Keep in your car. Scan when stopped. Pick best excuse. Escape ticket!

- ★ "Babysitter called...kid's throwing up."
- ★ "Dog's at pound...about to be zapped."
- ★ "Contact lens fell out...need safe place to stop."
- ★ Asthma attack! (Show empty inhaler).
- ★ "Late to funeral...need to deliver eulogy."
- ★ "Epileptic aunt needs pills ASAP!"
- ★ "Chasing truck that kicked up rock and cracked my windshield to get its plate number."
- ★ "My rare blood type is needed for dad's emergency surgery...he was in a crash."
- ★ "Watching friend's pitbull...loose in neighborhood."
- ★ "Trying to get home before pizza arrives."
- ★ "Oil warning light just came on...need gas station."
- ★ "Waterbed flooding house...need hose to drain."
- ★ Yank digital dashboard fuse. "Can't read speedometer...new fuse on order."
- ★ Steal pacifier from kid to prompt wailing.
- ★ "Thanks for stopping me. Where is...?"

REAL-TIME SPEEDTRAP ALERTS
e-mailed right to your cellphone—FREE!
CleanDrivingRecord.com

Speeding Excuse Cheat Sheet (cont'd)

Women Only

"Trying to get pregnant...I'm ovulating."

"Bladder infection...excruciating pain."

"Cycle just started...no spare tampons."

"Got off early...found husband cheating."

"Lost...late for babysitting job."

"Nipples just pierced...seat belt hurts."

"My lover's wife left for the night."

"Husband leaving for Air Force in half-hour."

"Boyfriend just proposed...too excited."

"Late to take pics of sister giving birth."

"I'm pregnant...dad's gonna kill me."

"Being chased by scary gang members."

★ "Left curling iron on."

Men Only

"Studying to be cop"...carry police textbooks.

"Late to pick up kids from ex."

"Trying to have a baby...wife ovulating right now!"

"Girlfriend leaving, must get to airport to propose.

"Girlfriend's pregnant...dad will kill me."

Wear sweatshirt from nearby PD.

Excerpted from *Speeding Excuses That Work* by Alex Carroll.

To order books, call **1-800-3-CAN-WIN** or visit *CleanDrivingRecord.com*

Subject: **Rock & Roll**
Date: Thurs, 25 Jan
From: Π. Σνψδερ<Σνψδερ22@ηομε.com >
To: copouts@copouts.com

If you've got any pre-existing front-end damage, such as a cracked headlight, paint nick or chipped windshield, give this one a try. Just explain to the cop that the car or truck in front of you just kicked up a rock onto your car, and you were trying to catch up to flag the guy down or get his license plate number. This one got me out of four tickets in a row!

Overheard At The Donut Shop

During a routine traffic stop, a police officer finds himself swatting at a fly that keeps circling his head. "What kind of dang fly is that anyhow?" he blurts.

The traffic offender replies, "That's a circle fly."

"I've never heard of a circle fly," says the officer.

"Well, circle flies are usually found circling a horse's ass," says the driver.

Enraged, the police officer says, "Are you calling me a horse's ass?"

"No sir," says the driver, "but you can't fool a circle fly."

Subject: **Egghead Defense**
Date: Thurs, 26 July
From: Δαϖε Χυλλψ <χυλλψ@ηομε.com >
To: copouts@copouts.com

On the way to the Rose Bowl one New Year's Day, I was pulled over on I-210 for doing 70 in a 55. When I got the ticket, the CHP officer stated that he just got on the freeway and clocked me for a couple miles while I was in the fast lane.

I decided to fight the ticket, and as the day of the trial approached, I remembered what he said about clocking me from 4 lanes over. I studied a map of the freeway and confirmed the curve where he'd pulled me over. At the time, I had just finished a physics class at UCLA, and I recalled that angular velocity (designated by Omega) equals linear velocity squared divided by the radius of the curve. It's a fairly simple equation that looks like this:

$$WW = \frac{V^2}{R}$$

My contention was that the CHP matched my angular velocity, not my linear velocity (driving speed) as we curved along the freeway.

At the trial, I explained this to the judge, and went to

work on the chalkboard and set our angular velocities equal, like this:

$$\frac{V^2}{R} = \frac{V^2}{R}$$

As I talked through my defense, the judge was mesmerized by the explanation. He interrupted me and asked if what I was describing was the reason that in long distance track events, the outside lane runners start farther up the track than inside runners. Bingo! I explained that the CHP officer was driving a greater distance than I was, while our angular velocities were equal. He paced me thinking I was going 70, but I was actually going 55. So I set the board up like this:

$$\frac{(V)^2}{R} = \frac{(70)^2}{R}$$

I'd worked the math ahead of time and figured what the radius of the turn had to be on—and what radius I had to be on—to make my speed equal to 55. I was a little concerned that my 'estimate' may have been a little aggressive, but I decided that since there could be doubt about the actual radius, that would therefore ensure my innocence, it was legitimate. I solved the equation for my speed and wouldn't you know it: my speed worked out to be exactly 55 mph!

My girlfriend (now wife) was in the courtroom and told me later that a couple CHP officers sitting next to her were absolutely amazed by my defense. They were impressed with this college student who was schooling the judge in the concept of angular velocity.

Well, the judge was impressed, too. Even though the officer argued the I-210 curved the *other* way, making a case for me driving *faster* than 70 mph (if he'd done the math, I'd have been travelling over 100 mph!), I disagreed, and the judge dismissed the ticket, citing an outstanding defense on my part. To this day that's the only physics equation I remember. I guess those damn story problems in math aren't so bad after all....

Before You Hit The Road

(Excuses continued on page 103)

The Secret Ingredient

that makes all excuses work

This book is packed with all types of ticket excuses, some fabricated, some real—all creative. But what makes them work? Virtually all of them share one basic element:

They make the cop FEEL YOUR PAIN...

... your anguish, your agony, your distress, your predicament, your loss. Make no mistake about it ... this is psychological warfare—and your weapon is GUILT.

Unless you're a fellow cop, emergency worker, attractive female, or in some 'special group' that can wangle preferential treatment, guilt is your only friend ... so make the most of it.

Think about it...

★ The guy with the hose on page 24 whose waterbed is probably flooding the downstairs apartment RIGHT NOW...can the cop feel his pain? You bet.

★ The lady on page 104 who just started her period and realized her spare box of tampons is empty... the cop doesn't even want to *think* about feeling her pain.

★ The geezer on page 108 rushing home to his wife before he loses his first real erection of the year... FEEL THE PAIN!

★ The poor kid on page 148 who was trying to catch that really cute topless girl who'd just winked at him as she blew by...ANY guy can feel his pain.

★ The man on page 152 who has to communicate with the officer via a pad of paper because a botched operation left him unable to speak? Are you feeling the pain yet?

Your goal is to make the cop feel AWFUL if he writes you a ticket. You want to make him feel so bad, he'll have nightmares if he writes you up. *How?* You must crack through his outer defensive shell to reach his heart. Yes, cops do have them. Some are harder to find than others, but they all have them.

Look…it's really not that tough. Just pretend you are the cop. What would someone need to say to you to make YOU feel really sorry for them?

★ Start your story or excuse the moment he asks for your license and registration. Talk it up while you're getting them out.

★ Look directly into his eyes.

★ Plead your case with feeling and emotion (ladies: turn on the waterworks).

★ Look and act sad or distressed.

★ Be repentant.

★ Pile your reasons on.

★ If you have a clean driving record … tell him.

★ If you're poor and can't afford the ticket…tell him…and give him the whole sob story.

★ If your dad or husband is going to beat you if you get a ticket…tell him.

★ ALWAYS ask if he can make it a 'warning.'

★ Tell him you've never driven here before.

★ Say you're not sure what the speed limit is.

★ If he must write a ticket, ask if he could please reduce it to an equipment violation (he still gets a quota notch for these).

Half-hearted efforts—forget it! They'll probably get you in more hot water than if you'd kept your mouth shut and just taken the ticket. Commit to it...go the distance...and give it all you've got.

Drive safely...think quickly...act decisively.

You're More Likely To Get Stopped If...

★ **You drive in the fast lane.**

If you were a cop, which lane would *you* watch? A cop once told me that 80% of all speeding tickets are written to vehicles in the fast lane. Stay in the middle lanes whenever possible.

★ **You keep switching lanes.**

This does more than call attention to you—it tells cops you're an aggressive or reckless driver. Besides, the more lane changing you do, the higher your chances of ending up in a wreck. Pick a lane, and stay in it.

★ **You drive a flashy car.**

The flashier the car, the brighter the target. Traffic cops don't earn a lot of money, and some of them may resent that you (or your daddy) do. Save your Ferrari for flaunting around Beverly Hills or the Hamptons.

★ **Your radar detector is VISIBLE.**

Cops generally agree: a visible radar detector virtually guarantees you a ticket. So hide the cord or get a wireless model, install a separate power source (don't use the cigarette lighter), mount the antenna in your grille, cover the lights and mount the receiver out of sight.

★ It's the beginning or end of the month.

According to Sergeant James Eagan, "You have heard that cops have a quota system and that is, in some respects, quite true. The productivity of police is usually checked monthly. Because of this policy, the procrastinating cops often find themselves in a position that requires they 'catch up.' Their more aggressive brothers have written their tickets at the beginning of the month. The best day to travel is the 15th of any month and the worst days would be the first or last few days of a month."

Adds Eagan, "If you can avoid the day shift by travelling later in the day, then by all means, do so." His reasoning is simple. Cops write more tickets at the beginning of their shift than at the end. Eagan speaks from 20 years' experience as a New York State Trooper. He's written thousands of tickets. I'd pay attention if I were you.

★ Your car is brightly colored.

Which colors jump out at *you* in a lot full of cars? Candy apple red? Neon yellow? Certainly not forest green or asphalt gray. Some cops take me to task on this point ... I don't know why. Bright colors affect us all the same way. They GET OUR ATTENTION! You don't want a cop's attention. You want him to look right past you.

★ **You're not wearing a seatbelt.**

Many states have "primary enforcement seatbelt laws." This means cops can stop you just for driving without a seatbelt. In other states, cops can always tack on a seatbelt violation after they stop you for something else. Don't hand him an easy reason to stop you. Wear it. You'll probably live longer anyway.

★ **You are young.**

Sure it's discrimination…but that's the way it is. Everyone knows the general rule…the younger you are, the faster you drive. Try dressing older. Or gray your temples. Well, okay…never mind. Just keep a low profile.

★ **You are male.**

Sorry guys…just remember that, unless it's a female cop, he's one of you. That means you've got an inside track on his psychological makeup. Make the most of it. Other than that, just be sure you study this book…and try to blend in as much as possible.

★ **Your vehicle is stickered.**

Bumper or windshield stickers call extra attention to your vehicle. You also run the risk of offending the cop—especially if he disagrees with your point of view or doesn't like your favorite team or grunge band. And those "Back The Badge," "D.A.R.E." and "Don't Drink & Drive" stickers? Peel 'em off. They only signal that you're trying to influence him.

The exceptions? Jesus fish emblems, the *God Is My Co-Pilot* types, those repulsive *My Child Is An Honor Student at Snotgrass Elementary* stickers, and *My Other Car Is A Fire Truck* (or *Ambulance*) decals. According to Sergeant Eagan, the latter can actually result in cops looking the other way. Cops often give preferential treatment to other emergency workers. But if you get stopped, be ready with a good story to back them up...like, "My son wants to be a fireman when he grows up and I got that sticker to encourage him."

★ Your windows are dark tinted.

Got something to hide? That's what dark tinting says to the cops, and they don't like it.

★ You're alone in the car.

If you have witnesses in the car, a cop knows that if there's any problems, it's no longer just his word against yours. It's now his word against you, AND all of your passengers. The more people in your car... the less likely you are to be stopped.

★ You're alone on the road.

Travelling within a pack of cars makes it tougher for him to maneuver in behind you and single you out. But if you're all alone out in front...you're easy prey.

★ Your headlights are on during the day.

Many speeders drive with headlights on during the day to intimidate slowpokes up ahead. Cops know this, and often pay special attention to cars with headlights on in the daytime. Even if you have automatic daytime running lights, it's better to keep your lights off if possible. Instead, just flash your high-beams when necessary.

★ Stuff is hanging from your rearview mirror.

Garter belts, air fresheners, graduation cap tassels, crystals, fairies and ESPECIALLY fuzzy dice, all give cops an easy excuse to write "obstruction of view" tickets to fill their quotas. Although rare, they do get written.

★ Your car has any of these attention-getters:

It's raised. It's lowered. It sports flashy mag wheels. Oversized tires. Tiny low-rider tires. Bald tires. And personalized license plates that may offend a cop.

★ Your car is on parole from the junkyard.

Is it dented, rusted, Bondo-ed, and showing signs of falling apart? Is the windshield cracked? These signal the cop that you don't take care of things. Your brakes could be bad. Your lights may not work. Your registration could be expired ...maybe even your license, and your insurance is probably nonexistent. Very often, he's right. This makes you a high-percentage target—and an easy ticket.

★ Your tailpipe is spewing a noxious plume.

This guaranteed attention-getter makes you an easy

target. And you *deserve* a ticket too. Fix your rolling chimney or get it off the road.

★ Your exhaust sounds like an incoming Scud.

If you've modified your exhaust to attract hot chicks, beware. You'll most likely attract a lot of cops. Be ready for an entirely different type of screwing.

★ You sport dreds, tattoos nose rings and/or mirrored sunglasses.

Sure, it's profiling and discrimination, but you're making the statement ... "I do what I want, and I don't care if I fit in." This can be taken by some cops as a direct challenge to their power and authority. So weigh the consequences and choose your battles wisely. As for the mirrored sunglasses ... they are often accompanied by other standard equipment like pipes, bowls and bongs. Bear that in mind.

★ You stare at a cop.

Most people know better, but I occasionally encounter some moron who doesn't get it. Better to spend your time staring into the sun.

How To Spot A Cop Before He Spots You

If you didn't catch the one-hour special on The Learning Channel called "Speed Traps," watch it in reruns. Aside from the fact that yours truly was a featured expert, it showed just how much today's cops play "hide and sneak."

Your challenge: spot them before they spot you. This will save you the inconvenience of being stopped in the first place. Here are your clues:

★ Cops love to sit on freeway on-ramps, ready to zoom into the blind spot behind you. Glance over your shoulder every time you pass an on-ramp to avoid these ambushes.

★ Adjust your speed when you see oncoming traffic flashing their headlights. This is the courtesy signal for "Speed Trap Ahead." And if you pass a speed trap, be sure to warn others by flashing your headlights, too.

★ Beware of blowing by 18-wheelers. Cops will sometimes pace them, hiding from your view in front or on the opposite side. When you blow by— too late—the cop's already on your tail.

★ Watch when approaching a pack of cars from behind. There may be a cop in front of them.

★ Watch out on highways and freeways with bushes in the median. There are often numerous little nooks where the staties lie in wait.

★ Always keep an eye on your rearview mirror. If the traffic behind you suddenly slows way down, it could be a sign of trouble.

★ Also, you should constantly be scanning at least a quarter mile ahead of you, keeping an eye open for cops and speed traps.

★ In Florida, the highway patrol have been known to dress up as road construction workers, complete with hardhats and orange vests, set up fake constructions sites complete with Caterpillar tractors, and run radar traps right from the tractor. Hard to believe... but it's true.

★ In Massachusetts, they're known to clock speeders from balloons. Victims have protested the allegations were full of hot air. No kidding.

★ Other states use light aircraft for speed enforcement. They need wide open stretches of highway to use this method effectively. Watch for white lines painted on the roadside and regularly glance up through your moon roof.

★ It is rumored that Arizona is considering installing photo radar cameras in fake roadside cacti. No joke. Beware of suspicious cactus specimens too close to the road.

★ If you make use of toll-roads and you use the

speed passes or EZ passes, be aware that your time and distance are automatically logged by the computer when you enter and exit the road. There have been reports that they want to use this data to mail people speeding tickets. If this should ever happen ... read the "Camera Ticket" section and take 'em to court.

★ At night, drive at or near the speed limit. You can't see cops and it's safer anyway.

★ Resist the temptation to immediately speed up after a cop exits the freeway. They often get right back on ... and nail you. I've seen it done several times.

★ Cops love to park under bridges/overpasses. It's shady and they're very difficult to spot. Watch for brake lights in front of you.

★ There are places where cops can pace you from frontage roads that run parallel to the freeway. Then they jump on and chase you down. If you notice a cop on a frontage road beside you... adjust your speed accordingly.

★ Cops can pace you from in front as well as behind. Many will blow right by you hoping to lull you into speeding up after they've gone by. They'll get a little distance ahead of you and set the cruise control above the speed limit. If you keep pace with them, they've got you. Then they slow way down and pull in behind you. I know, I fell for it once.

Stay Under
The Radar—
How To Stealth
Your Detector

Are you among the crowd that always seems to get nabbed for speeding? Then don't pull out of your driveway without a radar detector. Just remember that cops hate 'em, and you'll get 'extra attention' if they catch you with one. The secret is to stealth your detector. Here's how:

★ **Don't mount it on your windshield or windscreen.**

Corded or cordless, most detectors require windshield mounting to give the built-in antenna a clear view of the road. If you already own a unit with a built-in antenna (that would be most of you), try mounting it to the ceiling above your head, as close to the driver's door as possible. At this angle, your antenna still has a pretty good view of the road, but a cop will have to crane his head up inside your car in order to spot it. If you've got a cloth headliner, try using Velcro. Vinyl? Superglue it up there. Hard shell plastic? Screw it in. But don't be tempted to clip it to your visor. It's too easy to spot.

If you're currently in the market for a radar detector, consider the models where the antenna is *separate* from the receiver. Just mount the antenna inside the grille on the front of your car—then stealth your receiver up under your dash. And see my recommendations on the next page for the best models.

★ Stash the power cord.

If you have a corded model, then you'll need to conceal the power cord. Try hiding it behind the molding that runs between your windshield and your driver's side door. A screwdriver and half an hour should do the trick.

★ Don't plug it into your cigarette lighter.

It's the first place cops look. Make the nominal investment to have a mechanic wire-in another power source. It's well worth it. Obviously, this doesn't apply if you have a wireless model.

★ Cover the lights at night.

Sure they're cool, but do you want to avoid tickets—or put on a neon light display a cop could spot from a football field away? Most newer units allow you to dim the lights or switch them off. If yours doesn't have this feature, consider blacking out the lights with electrical tape. Valentine owners may throw a fit … but ask yourselves, "Do you really want to call that much attention to yourself at night?" Start relying on the beeps and whistles and keep your eyes on the road.

Buying A Radar Detector

How do you know which detector is best for you? Easy. I'll tell you. But what's not so easy is...the answer keeps changing.

Every time the cops get a new frequency for their speed-measuring toys, a new wave of detectors hits the market. So instead of listing *today's* best models—and then watching them go obsolete in three months—come visit my website:

www.copouts.com

Click on the "Radar Detectors" button for the latest scoop on the best new detectors. I stay on top of this stuff, and I'm happy to pass the info along to you. And while you're there, sign up to get real-time speed trap alerts in your town, as well as the *Winning Ticket Excuse of the Week*, which I'll e-mail to you free! I'll also occasionally include alerts about new detectors and other information I'm sure you'll find helpful.

In any case, here's some things to consider ...

★ Radar detectors will not save you every time. They rely on picking up some of the scattered beam when the cop clocks someone else. If you're the only car on the road and the cop turns on his gun just to clock you ... you don't get a warning ... you get nailed.

★ On the other hand, that's not normally the case, and a good detector can warn you of approaching radar 2 miles in advance. That gives you plenty of time to adjust your speed.

★ Detectors are illegal in Washington D.C., Virginia and all Canadian provinces except Alberta and British Columbia.

★ Battery operated detectors eliminate the power cord but the batteries must be changed regularly or performance will suffer.

★ 1-in-5 dash mounted (portable) detectors are stolen every year

★ Permanent remote mounted units are virtually impossible to spot (when properly installed) ... much less steal. These are the ones where the antenna is separate from the receiver.

★ The laser detector feature on most models is meaningless. Hell will freeze over before you get an early warning from a laser detector. Laser beams don't scatter like radar's do. Which means that when it goes off, you're already toast.

★ Of the quarter million speed guns in America, only 5% are laser ... and nearly half of those are in Ohio.

★ The rest are comprised of the 3 bands of police radar: 50% — K band; 35% — Ka band; and 10% — X band.

★ X band is the one shared by burglar alarms and garage door openers. It causes all the false alerts that detectors give. Its usage by police is rapidly dwindling and many new detectors allow you to turn it off entirely so you don't have to listen to the chatter anymore.

★ If you want to escape laser, you'll need a laser jammer. There are a couple of very effective models on the market. They are illegal in a few states ... check the laws.

★ DO NOT buy a *radar* jammer. It is a FELONY to jam or attempt to jam police *radar*. The ones that work are illegal. The ones that claim "passive jamming" with an "FM chirp" have NEVER passed a Speedlabs test. I wouldn't waste my money.

My advice? If you're relying on a piece of trash $99 EconoBrand special...dump it. You're going to have to spend at least a couple hundred bucks to get a decent unit that does the job.

Which Cops Are *Least* Likely To Ticket You? Here's How To Tell...

Did you know the higher the rank of the cop who pulls you over, the less likely you are to get a ticket?

In fact, according to 29-year veteran Sergeant Jim Drinkwater, if you get stopped by an officer with a rank of lieutenant or above, your chances of getting a ticket are only about 15 percent.

When asked why, Drinkwater replied, "Because we have more important things to do than go to traffic court...like play golf."

As a public service, here are the 10 ranks of officers from the bottom up—and how to tell them apart:

★ **Deputy or Officer** ... Bottom rung of the ladder. He has *no insignia on his uniform other than his badge*...and he's the most likely to lighten your wallet.

★ **Senior Officer or Corporal** ... The next rung up. In addition to his badge, he has *2 stripes on his sleeve*. He's still dangerous, though. Watch out.

★ **Sergeant** ... He's got *3 stripes on his sleeve.* This guy's seen his share of traffic court. He's a little less likely to write you up.

★ **Senior Sergeant** ... *4 stripes on his sleeve.* This is Drinkwater's rank. He's probably not gonna write you up unless you do something really stupid.

★ **Lieutenant** ... Look for a *gold or silver bar pinned to his collar.* 85% of the time he—and the ranks that follow—will let you off with a warning.

★ **Captain** ... *2 gold or silver bars on his collar.*

★ **Commander** ... Wears *a gold or silver star on his collar.*

★ **Deputy Chief** ... *2 stars*

★ **Assistant Chief/Assistant Sheriff** ... *3 stars*

★ **Chief or Sheriff** ... *4 stars, and sometimes 5 if you're in a big city*

Drinkwater also noted that different agencies are more likely to ticket you than others. Here they are, from most to least likely:

★ **Highway Patrol/State Trooper** ... Writing tickets is pretty much all they do.

★ **Police** ... They have other duties and are somewhat less likely to cite you.

★ **Sheriff** ... Even less likely.

★ **State Police** ... Don't even carry ticket books.

How do you tell them apart? Just look at the badge: the agency will appear right on it...in big bold letters.

A **Deputy** or **Officer**
wears no other insignia
than a badge

Senior Officer or **Corporal**

Sergeant

Senior Sergeant

> ***Editor's Note:*** *Some agencies*
> *use horizontal stripes.*

Lieutenant

Captain

Commander

Deputy Chief

Asst. Chief or Asst. Sheriff

Chief or Sheriff

Jim also shared some other odds-maker information:

★ Female cops are MORE likely to write you up than their male counterparts.

★ The younger the cop, the MORE likely you'll get a ticket.

★ A cop who gets out of his cruiser *without* his ticket book in hand will give you a *warning* 70% of the time.

★ A cop who gets out of his cruiser *with* his ticket book in hand will give you a *ticket* 70% of the time.

★ If you get stopped by a rookie cop who is accompanied by his field training officer ... you will get a ticket 99.9% of the time.

★ Beware of tickets from National Park Rangers ...they are often heard in FEDERAL COURT!

Getting Stopped
What To Do.
What NOT To Do.

1. **Acknowledge that you see the officer.** The minute you see his lights, either nod or wave at him, letting him know he's got your attention. Turn on your signal to let him know you are in the process of pulling over. DO NOT slam on your brakes! This will infuriate him. If there's a car in the lane next to you, speed up and merge in front of that car as opposed to slowing down and cutting in behind him. Be sure to leave the cop room to follow in behind you.

2. **Find a safe place to pull over.** No center dividers (medians), bridges, tunnels or railroad crossings, please. Get as far off onto the shoulder or side of the road as you can. This will make it much safer for him to approach your vehicle...and earn you lots of brownie points.

3. **Turn off your engine and put your key on the dashboard.** Cops do not like to approach idling cars. Put him at ease that you won't drop it into second gear and floor it...taking his foot with you.

4. **Turn off your radio.**

5. **If you're smoking, put out your cigarette.** In the ashtray, stupid, not out the window.

6. **If you're chewing gum, ditch that too.**

7. **If it's dark out, turn on your dome light.** This courtesy allows him too see you and your movements clearly.

8. **Roll down your window.** Do not make him bang on the glass with his night stick.

9. **Wearing sunglasses? Take 'em off and set them on the dash.** He'll feel more at ease if he can make eye contact with you. And he won't be

instantly suspicious that you've been smoking something.

10. **Put your hands up on the steering wheel.** Let him see where your hands are at all times.

11. **Don't make any sudden moves and DO NOT get out of the car.** This is very threatening to a cop. Unless you want an irate cop pointing a gun at you and screaming "FREEZE," stay in your car.

12. **DO NOT go rummaging around in your glove box or purse looking for your license and registration.** For all he knows, you're getting a gun. You are much more likely to get a warning from a relaxed cop than an edgy one. Don't make him edgy.

13. **If seatbelts are required in your state—and you're not buckled in—don't be a moron and try to sneak it on after he's pulled you over.** Cops can spot a jiggling shoulder harness from 50 car-lengths away.

14. **Do not try to stash your radar detector.** This will virtually guarantee not only a ticket, but a complete search of your car. NOW is the time to properly conceal your detector. Not when you are stopped.

15. **Wait for the officer to come to your window.** This may take awhile if he's checking on your plates. Be patient and SIT STILL.

16. **Let him speak first.** Do not blurt out, "What seems to be the problem officer?" He'll tell you soon enough. When he asks for your license, registration, etc., tell him where they are FIRST. Then get them slowly. He will appreciate this gesture. Very few people do it.

17. **Answer all questions politely or apologetically.** You may be tempted, but arrogance, insolence, disrespect and other negative attitudes are just plain stupid. Look Einstein, this guy has a gun, a badge, a billy club and a ticket book. And you want him to let you go with a warning ... remember?

18. **Address him as "Officer."** Don't overdo it with the "sir" thing. It sounds too contrived. If you are able to identify his rank (see page 76), it may earn you extra brownie points to call him Sergeant or Captain if that's the case. Don't do this unless you're sure. The last thing you want to do is insult him by calling him a lower rank than he is.

GUILTY?
Should You
Ever Admit It?

This is a huge question. And the answer is: *it depends.*

This book is full of stories from people who came right out and admitted what they did—apologized profusely—and begged for a warning.

Very often this works. Most cops recommend it. They'll tell you honest people get warnings while evasive people get tickets.

But sometimes, regardless of your honesty, you're gonna get written up—and your self-incriminating statements are the nails in your coffin.

So how do you know when to plead for mercy and when to keep your mouth shut? Consider the following:

1. Are you guilty?

Did you really do what the cop says you did, or did he confuse you with somebody else and nab you by mistake? I'd fight this one all the way. I'd politely inform the officer that I disagreed with him and felt he just made an honest mistake, or perhaps his equipment malfunctioned. If he still wants to write me up, I wouldn't argue any further, but you can bet I'd be going to court (although I certainly wouldn't tell him). I'd keep my mouth shut and take the ticket.

2. Will you fight the ticket?

If you've never gone to traffic court and are among the 90 percent who wouldn't even think of going there, then I recommend you put everything you've got into your excuse. Grovel, plead, get on your knees, brown your nose, whatever it takes ... because you won't get a second chance.

3. Where's his ticket book?

If a cop approaches your car WITHOUT his ticket book in hand, it usually means he wants to give you a warning ... not a ticket. He is LOOKING for an excuse to let you go. So give it to him. But, be sure to let him speak first. Let him tell you why he stopped you. It may simply be to tell you your license plate is about to fall off. If you jump in with, "I'm so sorry I was speeding officer, I promise I won't do it again," he might just write you a speeding ticket you wouldn't have gotten if you'd only kept your mouth shut.

4. Are you far from home?

If you're normally a ticket fighter, but you don't relish the prospect of having to drive six hours to come back and fight this one ... you might want to opt for the excuse and pray he'll let you go.

5. How good is your excuse … *really?*

If all you can come up with is you gotta pee, and you can't sell it to him in a way that makes him believe you REALLY GOTTA PEE, then you oughta just button your lip. You've got a much better chance of beating the ticket in court.

6. What's his rank?

Is he a high-ranking cop or a highway patrolman or trooper? (How to figure this out: page 76) Just remember this rule of thumb: the higher the rank, the less he wants to give you a ticket. Why? He's got better things to do than go to traffic court. He'd rather give you a warning. So give him a good excuse to do just that. Again: let him tell you why he stopped you before you start making excuses.

7. Is he wearing sunglasses?

Know why cops hide behind sunglasses? Because they don't want you making direct eye contact with them. The reason? Sunglasses let them remain detached and emotionless while you beg and plead. A cop's eyes are the doorway to his heart and soul. When you can look right into his eyes and beg for forgiveness and plead for a warning, it has a much more powerful effect on him than you staring at a couple of cold mirrors.

8. What's his mood?

Bad mood? You're probably better off shutting your mouth and keeping your excuses to yourself. Good mood? He's much more likely to respond favorably to your excuse. Many cops will let you go if you can make them laugh (often easier said than done). Keep a quiver of fresh jokes ready, and use 'em if and when appropriate. Be sure to ask him if that's his policy before you start joking around. If you're a cute blonde ... tell a blonde joke. That'll really catch him off guard!

POP QUIZ:
Which Of These Trick Questions Would Trap You?

1. "Do you know why I stopped you?"

They teach this question to rookies the first day at police academy. It's designed to get you to admit to doing something unlawful. Be careful. Unless it's blatantly obvious why he stopped you, it's best to avoid incriminating yourself. Using the right tone of voice, try, "No officer, I'm really not sure why you stopped me."

2. "How fast do think you were going?"

If you were going at a reasonable speed with the flow of traffic, the best response might be, "I'm sorry officer. I was paying attention to the traffic and the road around me and I wasn't staring at my speedometer, and I'm not exactly sure how fast I was going."

However, if you were really cookin'—and both of you know it—you may be better off going right straight for the mercy plea.

3. "Do you always drive that fast?"

Talk about a speed trap! I'd probably handle this by replying, "That's not a very fair question officer. Of course I don't always drive at the same speed. The roads and traffic conditions are always changing."

Once again, a coy answer may not be in your best interest if you were flying low and you know he's got you.

4. "What's the hurry?" or "Running late?"

These questions are actually prompting you to give him an excuse ... fancy that! Give him the best one you've got. On the other hand, if you're trying to avoid incrimination and you weren't playing Mario Andretti, just say, "No hurry officer," or "No officer, I've got plenty of time."

5. "How much have you had to drink?"

Be very careful with this question. If the answer is nothing ... clearly state that up front. If you've had a glass of wine or a beer with dinner, tell him and be ready to blow into a breathalyzer. Any more than that, and you're better off keeping your mouth shut and letting him do the field sobriety test on you. If you pass, count your lucky stars. If you don't, get ready to call your attorney.

6. Mind if I have a look around?

This is one of those 'between a rock and a hard place' questions. In order for him to search your car,

he needs ONE of three things: (1) probable cause
(2) a search warrant (3) your permission. If he had
probable cause, he'd just start searching—no
questions asked. To get a search warrant, he'd have
to show a judge probable cause anyway. So why did
he ask? He needs your permission. You DO NOT
have to give it to him.

You could say, "No officer, I'd prefer that you didn't.
It's not that I have anything to hide, it's just that I
think it's important I do my part to preserve our
constitutional rights." If you word this properly, and
say it in the right tone of voice, you shouldn't have a
problem. But the cop could take offense and give
you a hard time … especially if you've got two-foot-
long dreds and you're driving an old VW bus with the
curtains drawn.

It's also fair to say that if you do grant his request,
he'll probably be more inclined to let you go with a
warning. Just be aware he might find something you
didn't even know was illegal and he could even "plant
evidence" if he's so inclined.

7. "Are you still living at this address?"

Each state has a grace period for notifying the Motor
Vehicle Department of a change of address, some
as short as 10 days. After that, you can be cited. So
be careful how you answer this question. Here are
two good options: "Yes sir," or "No officer, I just
moved last week. Let me give you the new
address...."

S M I L E !
You Just Beat A
Camera Ticket.
(Here's how...)

First the bad news: This is the one ticket where even the world's best excuse will do absolutely no good, because there's no one around to give it to. The camera takes your picture. The ticket is mailed to you. Period.

Now the good news: You *can* beat it. Here are the loopholes:

If you're married...

Many people are not aware that spouses cannot be forced to incriminate each other. It's called "spousal privilege," and it works just like the "attorney-client privilege." With this in mind, register your car in your wife's name and your wife's car in your name. This way, your tickets will get mailed to your wife—and your wife's tickets will get mailed to you. Most states require the driver of the vehicle to be identified in the photo. You will of course challenge the ticket on the grounds that the person behind the wheel is

---

Editor's Note: *Laws may be different outside the U.S.A.*

---

obviously not you. When they ask who it is, refuse to answer based on "privilege." Do not say "spousal privilege," just say "privilege." They can't do anything further. Their hands are tied. They KNOW it's your wife ... but they have to dismiss your case anyway.

Not married?

Your attorney can work this loophole for you. Since your attorney can't be forced to incriminate you, he can show up in court on your behalf and pull the same stunt. He'll say he "cannot identify the driver as being my client ... based on privilege." Since many camera tickets cost $300 or more—and many attorneys will do the deed for half that price—this can be a viable option.

Another note on camera tickets

Many jurisdictions classify tickets as criminal offenses (as opposed to civil). If yours is a criminal case, you have a constitutional right to confront and cross-examine (ask questions of) your accuser. Since your accuser is a camera ...and cameras don't come to court or answer questions...they have no case.

They may send a cop in to testify against you anyway. Each time he speaks, politely interrupt and say: "Objection your honor, that's hearsay. The officer was not present at the scene." Just like you've seen on TV, second-hand testimony is inadmissible. But only *you* can shut him down. If you don't, the judge will let him keep going.

SAFETY WARNING...

DO NOT take this in any way to mean I am encouraging you or anyone else to run red lights. I am not. I do not have a death wish!

But I am VEHEMENTLY OPPOSED to ALL forms of camera enforcement. Here's why:

1. They do not stop the offender at the scene of the offense.

Example: A drunk driver blows through a red light. Camera takes a picture. Two blocks later, he mows down a couple of kids. Two weeks later, he gets a ticket in the mail. Had that camera been a real cop, those two kids would still be alive. Think about it.

2. Special circumstances are impossible to determine.

Example: You're waiting to make a left-hand turn at a green light (no arrow). Your car is hanging in the middle of the intersection. Another car right behind you is waiting to turn as well. Traffic is heavy, with no breaks in the oncoming cars. The light turns yellow. Traffic keeps coming. The light turns red. Two stragglers from the opposite direction run the red light. Finally, you're able to safely complete your left-hand turn. Flash. The camera goes off. Did it record the whole sequence of events? Of course not. Would a real cop write you a ticket? Highly unlikely.

3. Cameras reduce the deterrent of actual police presence.

It's too easy for law enforcement agencies to fall into the trap of relying on cameras to do their job. The fact is, a camera can never be a substitute for a real police officer.

★ Cameras see events in black and white, unable to evaluate a series of events and make a subjective decision based on the situation.

★ Cameras are unable to engage in 'positive enforcement.' (When a cop just issues a warning to someone who makes an honest mistake.)

★ Cameras are not a deterrent to drunk, impaired or inattentive drivers. Real cops are.

4. They are run by PRIVATE companies for PROFIT!

This is more than an obvious conflict of interest—it's illegal and unconstitutional as well. For example, multinational aerospace manufacturer Lockheed-Martin has been one of the major manufacturers and sponsors of camera enforcement programs. Here's what happens behind the scenes:

★ Because the units are so expensive, most cities contract with the manufacturer, giving them a hefty percentage of all fines collected.

★ In exchange, the manufacturer installs the cameras at no charge to the city.

★ Because these cameras are highly sophisticated and require technical staff to operate, most cities also authorize the private company to operate and maintain the cameras—even mail out the tickets!

Law enforcement for profit, controlled by private enterprise—is a recipe for disaster.

5. And now they're SHORTENING THE YELLOW LIGHTS to maximize ticket revenue!

This is where the truth comes out. This will really make your blood boil.

Here are the facts, from a report by Tait & Cusack:

★ Beginning in 1998, the City of San Diego contracted for the installation of 19 red light cameras. With much fanfare, they proclaimed these cameras would be installed at intersections with high accident fatality rates in the hopes of preventing accidents and saving lives.

★ What *really* happened? NOT ONE of the 19 intersections where the cameras were eventually installed was on the city's list of high-accident intersections for the previous two years.

★ Records indicate that many potential inter-sections were rejected because the yellow light was TOO LONG, resulting in low violation volume.

Wait. It's gets better…

★ After the red light camera program began in San Diego, at least two intersections had their yellow lights SHORTENED by a full second BEFORE the cameras were installed! Can you believe this?!

★ Traffic engineering studies determined long ago that for SAFETY, a yellow light must last at least one full second for each 10 mph of speed limit on that road. This allows people travelling at the speed limit the time they need to come to a safe stop.

★ Now get this: ELEVEN of the cameras were

placed at intersections where the yellow light was only 3 seconds long—even though the speed limits there ranged between 35 and 50 mph. Those yellow lights should have been set at durations ranging between 3.5 and 5 seconds. No wonder some of these cameras were raking in over $500,000 a month—people couldn't stop in time!

★ Due to this poor yellow light timing, accident rates actually INCREASED at many of these intersections.

★ The LIES that were spread about the cameras reducing "red light runners" by 45% were based on ONE intersection where technicians INCREASED the yellow light time from 3 to 4.7 seconds. The camera had NOTHING to do with the reduction in "red light runners"—it was the increased yellow light time.

These cameras are cash cows for cities and the private corporations they contract with—and now they're injecting them with steroids by shortening the yellow lights to make even MORE money.

6. They encourage dangerous intersections.

Because of the profit motives involved, the presence of cameras can cause poor engineering and bad light timing to be totally ignored, and even exploited. This does not make our roads safer.

Overpaying The Fine:

Does It Work?

If you already know this technique, skip to the next paragraph. If not, here's how it's supposed to work. You get a ticket. You mail in your check for the fine, plus a couple of bucks extra. The court then supposedly sends you a small refund check for the amount you overpaid. But you don't cash it. Instead, you tear it up and throw it away. This supposedly leaves your case open indefinitely, preventing it from ever showing up on your driving record.

Sounds good, doesn't it? Yet I've never seen any

tangible proof it has ever worked for anyone. Virtually everyone I've spoken with who tried it said the court just kept the extra money, and the ticket showed up on their record anyway. One account has this "urban legend" starting in Australia back in 1998. Did it ever work there? I have no idea. But it has circulated around the internet more times than I care to count.

For years now, every time the subject has come up when I've been on the radio, I've asked if anyone out there actually succeeded at this technique. I've easily posed the question to hundreds of thousands of people. Know how many 'yes' responses I've gotten? Two. A couple of guys in the New York City area claimed they'd succeeded—several years ago. All other New York City area respondents said the tactic had failed.

My guess is that even if those two guys were telling the truth (I never saw the refund checks), the loophole has long been closed.

If I were you...I wouldn't do it.

But if you've ever been successful at this ... let me know...and send me proof: a copy of your ticket, the refund check, and your driving record.

Editor's Note: Rumor has it the courts themselves may have actually started this racket ... and even set up a special fund for all the overpaid fines ... with proceeds going to buy more radar guns!

Sexual Harassment During Traffic Stops:
Safety Tips For Women

Regretfully, I must include this section—a very real issue today. Let me share a story with you.

I recently moderated a radio talk show on WOR in New York on the subject of sexual harassment by police. There had just been a rash of cases and reports of Long Island police stopping solo female motorists at night and sexually abusing them. I was asked to inform female listeners about their rights in traffic stop situations.

After a brief recap of cases in the news, the host opened the phones to any women who'd ever had similar experiences. Instantly the lines jammed with women—young and old—sharing horrifying stories. Many had never told a soul. All said they were afraid. Their voices shook. Some cried. The accounts were appalling. We were both shocked. After the segment, the lines were still jammed.

I had no idea this type of sexual harassment was so widespread. So I decided to include the following safety tips to help women stay safe:

★ **Try not to drive alone at night**...especially in rural areas. Nearly all cases I've heard of occurred under these conditions.

★ **DO NOT STOP FOR UNMARKED CARS**... Instead, drive quickly and safely to a populated, well lit area. If it's a real cop, he'll probably call for backup. This is good. You are much less likely to face harassment if five cops are there. Calmly explain your fears and your actions, and the situation should diffuse quickly. If he's not a real cop...you may have saved your life.

★ **Drive to a well lit populated area to stop**... even if you're stopped by a real police car. Once again, the officer may call for backup. Once again...the more cops, the better.

★ **Do not dress provocatively**...If you must travel alone at night, four-inch pumps, a red miniskirt and tight halter top are asking for trouble. Dress down, put your hair up in a baseball cap and take off your makeup...especially the red lipstick. Look as plain and unsexy as possible. You could also keep a long coat in your car to cover-up with ... for those occasions when dressing down is not an option.

★ **Keep your cell phone handy**... If you are signaled to pull over, and you do choose to stop, call a friend to tell them what's happening and where you are. They could be a witness if anything happens. Then, don't hang up, but set the phone on the seat next to you so they can hear everything that's said. If you have a hands-free system in your car, that's even better.

★ **Alternately, you can call 911**...and tell the dispatcher where you are and ask her to listen in (many night dispatchers are women, so she'll understand). If something goes awry, she may be able to get somebody quickly to the scene.

★ **Open your window a crack**...as opposed to my normal traffic stop recommendations, do not roll down your window all the way.

★ **Turn off your engine, but leave the keys in the ignition.**

★ **LOCK YOUR DOORS.**

★ **If you feel threatened in any way, DO NOT GET OUT OF YOUR CAR**...no matter what he says. Politely refuse, and tell him if he wishes to detain you, he can follow you to the nearest police station. Ask him for directions and even invite him to call for backup. If you've got a cell phone, call 911 and tell the dispatcher you want someone waiting outside the police station when you arrive.

★ **Always be polite, but firmly explain your fears**...if he's a good cop, he'll understand. If he starts getting agitated, that may indicate he had ulterior motives for stopping you—and you're doing the right thing.

Be careful. Stay alert. And follow your instincts.

"But Officer, I Just Found Out I'm Pregnant!"

★ **PMS**...Most all cops know THIS story because they deal with it at a personal level every month. And most are smart enough just to leave you alone. Start by apologizing for your PMS, and then start bitching about cramps, headache, husband, etc. Most cops can't wait to get away from this!

★ **Bladder Infection**...Once again, most cops have personal experiences with this. Just apologize profusely while agonizing over your pain, and you'll probably be on your way shortly thereafter.

★ **Period**...According to one officer (who wished to remain anonymous), this is the single best excuse a woman can use. He says, "When the male officer approaches, she needs to be distressed and remorseful about the speed. Then say something like, 'I'm so sorry I was speeding, I forgot my tampons and I'm having a VERY heavy day (don't sterilize it). I know it's no excuse to speed, but I'm a mess and I need to get home to change my clothes before it goes through

—please don't ask me to get out of the car because I'm afraid if I stand up...." He adds, "Most male officers will have sent you on your way before that point."

★ **Pregnant**...You are coming from the clinic—or maybe you just took one of those drug-store EPTs and it was positive. It shouldn't be too difficult to muster a great deal of distress—even panic. If you are young, be sure to capitalize on the "Ohmygod, daddy's gonna KILL me" factor. If you really want results, be sure to mention that your daddy is a preacher or priest.

★ **Ovulating**...Say this with wide-eyed enthusiasm: "I've been trying to get pregnant for months. My doctor told me the INSTANT I feel like I'm ovulating —go home and have sex! I just called my husband who is on his way so I've got to be going right NOW!"

★ **Cheating Mate**...This event would call for a little "hysteria." Most women are good at this—and most guys CANNOT handle it. For emphasis, hyperventilate as you explain how you'd just gotten off work early to come home to find your mate in bed with your best friend—only minutes earlier.

★ **Drying Hair**...More than one woman has escaped by telling the officer that she hadn't had time to dry her hair before leaving for work. So she'd rolled down the windows to let the air flow do the job. Be sure to apologize for not paying attention to your speed.

★ **Being Chased**...This one is so easy for women to pull off. Just make up your favorite bad guy. Then hysterically explain to the officer that the really scary, psycho, bad guy or guys were chasing you and you were afraid for your safety. The more you embellish how bad these gang member types looked, the better. Make sure you have a good description of a suspicious vehicle and a partial license plate number to further validate your story.

★ **Abusive Husband**...Several women claimed this worked very well for them. "Please don't give me a ticket officer. Please, please, please!!! My husband will beat me if I get a ticket. Oh god no, no—I can't bear it any more." Most cops are very sensitive to this because they have to deal with domestic violence all the time and they're not going to be too excited about exacerbating it

★ **Left Curling Iron On**...It's easy to pull this one off...just act like an airhead. Say you think you left it sitting on a towel...thus the rush. Most cops will just walk away shaking their heads. (A guy could actually use this one, too. Just explain that your wife or girlfriend just called from work to say she 'thinks' she left it on... sending you into a panicked race home to see if there still IS a home!)

★ Boyfriend Just Proposed

...A happy one for a change. You should be elated, even hysterical—and cooing over the engagement ring sitting on your finger. No cop in his right mind is going to ruin your special moment. Be sure to be apologetic for not paying attention and plead for a warning.

★ **Just got pierced**... Say with a pained expression: "I just had my nipples pierced and the seatbelt really hurts! I'm trying to get to the drugstore to get some painkillers!" This can definitely get you out of a seatbelt citation—and probably a speeding ticket, too.

★ **Quickies**... "I'm on the way to my lover's house. His wife just left and I rarely get such a great opportunity and I promise I won't ever speed again!"

OR..."It's my husband's birthday, and I need to get home to give him an 'oral favor' before all the party guests arrive!"

Subject: **Lucky Stiff**
Date: Fri, 2 March
From: Αχεχο <αχεχο@ηομε.com >
To: copouts@copouts.com

It is embarrassing, but it is the truth. I was experiencing my first "rise" in quite some time, so I phoned the missus and told her I'd be home real soon! I was only one exit from the house when a young patrolman stopped me.

So when he comes up to my window, I summoned all my courage and explained that I had my first stiffy in months, and that the missus was expecting me any minute. He just turned beet-red and waved me on. I thanked him and barreled on home. (You can use my story, but please don't give out my name.)

Subject: To Pee Or Not To Pee
Date: Thurs, 1 March
From: Μεεσε <γδμεεσε@ηομε.com >
To: copouts@copouts.com

One busy weekend while out driving with the family, I drove by a motorcycle cop with a laser gun at 57 mph in a 35 zone. With my brain traveling at the speed of light, I came up with what I believed to be an ingenious plan.

My daughter—at an age where she repeats everything like a parrot—was in the backseat. I told my wife that when we stop, to jump out, grab our daughter and run into the restaurant bathroom as fast as she can. Then, as we turned into the parking lot to stop, I just kept repeating to my daughter, "Daddy gotta pee, gotta pee."

As the cop walked up to the car, he saw my wife urgently removing our daughter from her car seat as she was spouting, "Daddy gotta pee, gotta pee." All I said was "SORRY. She is just out of diapers and this car is only 3 weeks old!" All he said was, "I have kids, too—and I hope you can drive a little slower from now on."

Subject: **Officer PLEASE...**
Date: Wed, 23 May
From: ☐Δαπιδ Γαρ <δαπιδ@ηομε.com >
To: copouts@copouts.com

"I'm trying to get to my child's daycare, but they just called and said (s)he...

☑...has a high fever and needs to be picked up now! They won't allow a child with a fever to stay on the premises for fear of liability and infecting other kids."

☑...had a seizure! It's over now, and they said (s)he seems okay, but I'm scared and so is my child."

☑...fell off the monkey bars and banged her/his head! They don't seem to think it's serious enough to go to the hospital, but you just don't know till you get there."

☑...fell down the steps and broke off a tooth! There's a lot of blood, and my child is crying."

☑...got in a fight and spit on another child on the playground! I raised her/him better than that, and this requires swift discipline."

☑...has been evacuated! Someone smelled gas in the building and there's no one else who can pick her/him up, so I'm trying to get there as soon as possible."

Subject: **Roll On**

Date: Sun 8 April

From: Σολομαν <ΤΚΔΣολ@ηομε.com >

To: copouts@copouts.com

I got a ticket for rolling through a stop sign at the top of a steep hill. I truly did roll through the stop sign—everybody else does, too, because it makes no sense to stop there. Anyway, the cop didn't give me a chance to give him an "excuse," so I took it to court.

I told the judge I was relatively new at driving a stick and I'd actually stopped, but when I went to go forward, I began rolling back. I'd started to panic that I would roll into the person behind me, who was now moving forward. So once I got going, I kept going. When the judge asked the officer if this was possible, he said yes—and I got off without a ticket.

I am a professional photographer, but you don't need to be a pro to pull this off. When a cop stops you, tell him, "My sister is having her first baby and I'm trying to get to the hospital to take pictures of the birth." It's advisable to have a good camera (or simply a good camera case) on the seat. A sense of urgency is a good idea, too. If the cop is unmoved by your story, add in, "She just conquered ovarian cancer and by pure miracle she was able to carry a child, and I promised to take the photos." Still unwavering? Pour it on: "She went into labor two weeks early and caught me off guard so I really need to get there so I don't miss the birth and ruin it for my sister." And the capper: "If you're going to give me a ticket, please just do it, but I've REALLY got to go!"

Subject: Dumb Looks
Date: Thurs, 28 June
From: Δ Ωαψνε<Σεδφεμεμ@ηομε.com >
To: copouts@copouts.com

While riding my 650 Triumph Bonneville, I was pulled over by the Washington state patrol. "Your motorcycle's too loud," said the cop. "How loud IS it?" I replied. Dumb look. Then I said, "Let me see the reading on your decibel meter." Another dumb look. Feeling quite brazen, I asked, "What is the noise level for this size engine?" He replied, "Well, what size is it?" I said, "A 650." Yet another dumb look. "Well," he said, "it's just too loud" and he wrote me a ticket.

When I went to court, he told the judge his story, and I told him mine (minus the smart remark, of course). The judge asked him what the level was on the decibel meter (which cops here don't carry) and he gave the judge that same dumb look. The judge threw out the ticket, but there's more.

I took that cop to Small Claims Court. They said I couldn't sue the State Patrol, but I informed them I wasn't suing the State Patrol, but him, personally, for harassment. I won a day's wages plus court costs, and he got a reprimand from the judge. I haven't seen that cop on the roads since!

While driving on Highway 580 in Pleasanton, CA in my newly purchased Ford Ranger pickup, I was clocked by a CHP aircraft doing 75 mph in a 65. A motorcycle officer—who did not witness the violation—stopped me and wrote the ticket after communicating with the aircraft.

I went to court, pled not guilty, and requested a court trial. I subpoenaed the motorcycle officer, the pilot, and his copilot. All three showed up in court.

Dressed in a nice suit and tie, first I examined the motorcycle officer, getting him to admit he did not see the violation, but was acting on information given to him via the radio from the aircraft. Then I examined the copilot, getting him to say he sits next to the pilot, and uses a stopwatch or clock, charts, ground markings and verbal information from the pilot. Then I examined the pilot, and got him to admit five very important things. First, that he flies the aircraft. Second, he has to locate each vehicle on the ground. Third, he has to note the speed of his aircraft. Fourth, he has to locate ground markings, and fifth, he then communicates this

information to his copilot. I had been cited at 5:43 pm and traffic was extremely heavy, just like every day at rush hour on the 580. *Now comes the good part.* I asked the pilot how many white pickup trucks would be on Highway 580 at around 5:45 pm on a weekday during rush hour? Of course, he had no idea. I then asked if he thought there was more than one ordinary plain white pickup on the 580 during rush hour. After several minutes of questioning, the officer admitted there probably was more than one ordinary plain white pickup on the freeway at that time. Then I went for the kill: after reminding him that he had already testified to doing five things as he flew the aircraft, I said, "Well, if you're doing all those things while flying—including taking your eye off my vehicle for a few seconds while locating your ground markings and determining the speed of your aircraft—then how do you know you kept my vehicle in sight at all times?" He admitted that he did take his eye off my vehicle for a short period of time. I continued, "With more than one white pickup truck on that freeway, you may have had the motor cop stop the wrong vehicle. Isn't that right, officer?" Well.....I WON!!! The judge said I put a "slight doubt" in the court's mind, and that's all you need for an infraction case. People were asking if I was a lawyer, and if I'd handle their cases, too!

Here's one that should work on any cop, male or female. When I get stopped for speeding, I say that my wife and I have been trying to get pregnant for many months. Since the doctor told us that the INSTANT she feels like she's ovulating—we need to have sex right away.

And now the three magic words that should get you out of a ticket every time: "She just called!"

Subject: **Ex-cused!**
Date: Fri, 27 April
From: ϑερομε Π <φερομεΠ2@ϖεριζον.com >
To: copouts@copouts.com

My excuse when I get pulled over is to state (with my eyes bulging out of my head) that I'm in a hurry to pick up my kids because if I am late my &%$#@*! ex-wife will not let me take my kids. You know why this works so well? Because so many cops are divorced.

Overheard At The Donut Shop

Two rednecks are driving down the road drinking a couple of beers. Bubba says, "Lookey thar up ahead, Earl, it's a police roadblock! We're gonna get busted fer sure!"

"Don't worry, Bubba. We'll just pull over and finish, then peel off the labels and stick 'em on our foreheads." "What fer?" asks Bubba. "Just let me do all the talkin'" says Earl.

When they're done with the beers, they toss out the bottles and put a label on each of their foreheads. As they reach the roadblock, the sheriff says, "You boys been drinkin'?"

"No, sir!" says Earl, pointing at the labels. "We're on the patch."

Subject: **Fond Farewell**
Date: Tues 6 Feb
From: Βεννιε Μιγ<BBϖαμπ@ηομε.com >
To: copouts@copouts.com

My husband was my excuse, but this can work for you since so many women now serve: "I'm trying to get to the Federal building downtown because my husband is leaving for the Air Force and I only get a half hour with him and I won't see him again for three months!"

Overheard At The Donut Shop

A driver was pulled over by a police officer for speeding. As the officer was writing the ticket, she noticed several machetes in the car.

"What are those for?" she asked suspiciously.

"I'm a juggler," replied the man. "I use them in my act."

"Well, show me," the officer demanded.

So the driver took out the machetes and started juggling them, first three, then more, finally seven at one time, overhand, underhand, behind the back, putting on a dazzling show and amazing the officer.

Another car passed by. The driver did a double take, and said, "My God. I've got to give up drinking! Look at the test they're giving now."

Subject: **Proof Switcheroo**
Date: Fri, 10 Aug
From: □Στεωε Τ <ιαμνοτχυρρεντ@ηομε.com >
To: copouts@copouts.com

I was traveling down the George Bush Tollway in Dallas at about 80 MPH. As I come around a curve, a state trooper—going in the opposite direction—swings his vehicle down into the grassy partition between the tollway and does a classic dirt-in-the-air Dukes of Hazard U-turn to go after me.

As the officer comes up to my window, he asks if this is my car. "Of course it is officer, but it just so happens that you can't pull up the information, because this is a company vehicle," I say. That bug-eyed trooper tells me he pulled me over for speeding, and asks for my proof of insurance. Now this is where my plan comes in.

I do have valid insurance as well as a valid registration, but I give him the old ones instead. "These are expired," he says. So I ask if he would just cite me on that and let the speeding go as a warning, since I couldn't afford to pay the ticket. He agrees, and I zoom on down the road knowing full well that all I have to do is show the current proofs to the court clerk —saving that fine AND the $150 speeding ticket!

Subject: **Road Rageous**
Date: Mon, 25 June
From: ▢Π.Στυρμερ <Παυλ∑@ηομε.com >
To: copouts@copouts.com

I was safely doing 70 mph in a 55 zone, just like everyone else on the highway, when this cop pulls me over. My heart was pounding and my palms were sweating because my wife (and insurance agent) would kill me if I got another ticket, when this amazing idea hit me: why not use my high anxiety to my own advantage???

The instant the cop reached my window, I pointed to the first car that happened to pass by and blurted out, "There! THERE! That white Maxima. [gulp!] I don't know what I did to him, but that crackpot was following me close and yelling and flipping me off. He nearly hit my bumper on the on-ramp!" And then—to seal the deal—say, "THANK YOU FOR PULLING ME OVER, officer. You saved me from a wild case of road rage!"

Well, he let me go and told me to drive safely. As I pulled away, I saw him radioing something to his fellow officers. I know I wouldn't have wanted to be driving a white Maxima THAT fine day.

Subject: **Inflatio**

Date: Fri, 27 July

From: ΑντηονψΑ <ΑντηονψΑ@αολ.com >

To: copouts@copouts.com

After crossing the double yellow line several times on a curvy road, I got pulled over because the officer thought I was intoxicated. I had not been drinking, but I had been talking to my friends in the car and not paying close attention to the road.

I told the officer I had overinflated my front tires by mistake, which made the steering way too loose, and I was just about to pull over to release some of the air.

My friends did a good job trying not to laugh, and the officer told me to be careful and then let me go.

Subject: **It's All In The Wrist**
Date: Thurs, 7 June
From: ☐Λεωισ <Λεωισ184@αολ.com >
To: copouts@copouts.com

After my wife delivered our son a few years back, I dashed out of the hospital to run a few errands. When a cop pulled me over for speeding, I acted very worried (I was!) as I explained I had to get back to the hospital because they just called and said something was wrong with my newborn. I flashed the hospital wristband and the cop said, "Remember, it's more important to get there safely than it is to speed and end up with a bed of your own. So just be careful and I hope everything turns out okay."

Now I simply keep that hospital wristband in my glovebox and slip it on whenever I get pulled over.

Subject: **The $5 Excuse**
Date: Thurs, 7 June
From: ☐Λεωισ <Λεωισ184@αολ.com >
To: copouts@copouts.com

If you go on the internet, you can easily buy a medic ID bracelet for less than five bucks. And the best part? They never ask if you truly need it. Mine says I am diabetic. I just keep it in my pocket and if anyone asks why, I say it chafes my wrist. If I ever get pulled over, I apologize to the policeman, and tell him I am in a hurry to get home to get my insulin. A couple of times they've asked if I needed an ambulance, to which I simply replied, "Not yet, but I might if I don't hurry!"

Subject: **Top Banana**
Date: Sat, 8 Aug
From: ΡιχιηΕΡιχη <ΡιχηιεΡιχη@ηομε.com >
To: copouts@copouts.com

I was late for a meeting and starting to grow very hungry—with a few miles still to go through town. Luckily, I had a banana left over from breakfast, so I peeled it using one hand and my teeth, while driving carefully with the other hand. I was happily eating my banana when suddenly—without warning—I let loose a sneeze that sent a major mouthful of mashed banana spewing across the inside of the windshield in front of me. At that very same moment, I noticed I'd run a red light. And the very next moment, I realized I was being pulled over.

When the cop got to my window, I said I honestly didn't see the red light. The cop wanted to know how on earth I could miss a traffic light, and I showed him: the spray of partially digested banana spew actually obscured my vision. That poor cop made a face like I'd turned his stomach inside out. He told me to wipe it off and keep going—and not to eat while I was driving.

Subject: **Hand Job**
Date: Thurs, 5 April
From: Τροψ Βροων <τBροων29@αολ.com >
To: copouts@copouts.com

I was given a ticket for changing lanes without a signal, and I pleaded innocent. When I went to court, I asked the officer how he knew I did not use a signal.

"I saw you," he replied.

So I said, "You mean you were focused on the rear of my vehicle throughout the entire lane change?"

"Yes," he replied.

Then I went for the kill. "Well then, that would explain why you did not see my arm hanging out of my window, signaling the turn."

The officer was speechless and the ticket was dismissed.

Subject: **Hi-Testosterone**
Date: Thurs, 26 April
From: Δεννισ Η <δεννιση67@ηομε.com >
To: copouts@copouts.com

I was working at a local supermarket, stocking shelves over summer break. One Saturday night, I got a call from one of the girls I worked with—she had something she wanted to give me at her house that night. We'd already been intimate, so I instantly thought I was about to get lucky again.

She lived right near work. You'd just make a right out of the parking lot, drive straight for 4 blocks, make another right, cross an intersection, and her house is on the corner. As I was making that second right, a cop pulled me over. He asked why I was speeding down a suburban street, tailgating, not using my blinker, not stopping at the stop sign, and while he was at it—not wearing a seatbelt? I handed him my PBA card along with the other credentials. He handed back the PBA card, and told me I was going to have to give him another story because the PBA card wasn't going to work.

"Look officer," I said. "When I was at work, this girl called and asked me to come over. I think I'm going to get lucky tonight!" He replied, "Okay, I'll let you go,

but if I see you blow that red light at the next intersection, I'm going to pull you over again."

"That's okay officer," I said. "Her house is right there on the corner, I won't even go through it."

"You're going right there to the white house on the corner?" he asked. "Who is the girl?"

"Sue Jones*," I replied.

He then walked back to his police cruiser, and came back 6 minutes later with a summons for not wearing my seatbelt, blowing through the stop sign, and driving fast down a suburban street. He handed them to me and said, "I'll see you in about an hour. If you and my daughter are downstairs in the living room and not up in her bedroom, I'll forget about these." He handed me the tickets and walked back to his car. Needless to say, I didn't go over to her house for fear of seeing her father later that night.

* Name changed to protect the innocent.

Subject: Foreign Matter

Date: Fri, 27 July

From: ☐ΠετερΟ <πokωερ@υμβχ.edu>

To: copouts@copouts.com

Because I spent half my life in Europe, I have an international driving license issued in Austria. I still visit the country often, so I keep the license up to date. I also have an American driver's license.

On three occasions in the past year and a half, I have been pulled over in the U.S. while driving a friend's car. When the officer requests my license, I give it to him—the international one. The look on their faces says it all. They are clueless! They can't even send a

ticket to the address on the paperwork, because I say I'm about to leave the country. All they ever do is issue me warnings, saying "this is not how we drive in the U.S." I count on this working till I meet the same cop twice.

Subject: **Dead Ringer**
Date: Sat, 7 April
From: ☐Δ Ηυϕϕμαν<<u>δηυϕϕμαν@ηομε.com</u> >
To: copouts@copouts.com

This actually happened to my parents, but if you play your cards right, it can work for you. One day, my parents (who are always running late) were actually late driving to my grandfather's funeral. When they got pulled over, my father apologized politely to the officer and said although he knew he was speeding, he had to get to the funeral in time so "my wife can deliver the eulogy for her father." *Bam!* No ticket.

> ***Editor's Note:*** *Keep a handwritten eulogy stashed in your center console.*

 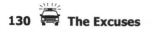

Subject: **Red Menace**
Date: Sat, 21 July
From: ϑαχκP<ϑαχκρ@αολ.com >
To: copouts@copouts.com

My friend and I were clipping along in a '73 Mustang convertible with the top down—white leather interior gleaming in the sun, music blasting, life grand. The speed limit on the road was 35 mph and I was hitting somewhere about the 50 mark. Of course, a cop emerged from nowhere with his lights a blazin' to chase the two women in the hot red Mustang.

When he walked up to my window, I gave him a shocked look of horror and exclaimed that my friend was having a "feminine hygiene emergency" and we were racing to her house to remedy the situation.

My friend sure played her part: she crossed her legs and looked very panicked. The policeman's face went from me to her, down to the white leather seats—then back up to me again. He very quickly told me to pay more attention, be careful, and get on my way. No ticket, no warning—a complete escape!

Subject: **Booby Trap**
Date: Thurs, 26 July
From: ϑεαννινε<Γφαγ@ηομε.com >
To: copouts@copouts.com

I was driving to the beach one day in my brand new Camaro, when I made an illegal turn and suddenly I had a police car behind me. He seemed to come out of nowhere. Anyhow, since I was on my way to the beach, I was wearing my bikini top, and when the cop came to my window, of course the first thing he looked at was my chest. So he asked me the usual questions about did I know the turn was illegal and yada yada yada. Then he asked me where I was going.

Well, I told him I was heading towards the bay to take an afternoon cruise on my "yacht." So I smiled and asked, "Would you like to join me?" knowing darn well he couldn't. I told him where my "yacht" was docked and we set a time to meet. He was thrilled! Needless to say, he let me off the ticket and REALLY looked forward to seeing me on my "yacht." I guess my boobs got me off the hook that day!

Subject: **Calibrate THIS!**
Date: Mon, 6 May
From: ☐Αρτ Μιλβυτα <μιλβυτα@ηομε.com >
To: copouts@copouts.com

When I got pulled over for doing 44 in a 35, I told the cop I'd been watching my speed very closely, and was ABSOLUTELY SURE I was going 35. "Do you suppose there's a chance my speedometer might be off?" I asked. "Well, *uhhh,* it's always a possibility," he replied. Then it hit me. "Gosh, I'd really like to know if my speedometer is reading the wrong speed," I said, scratching my head. "If I turn around and go back, could you clock me to see how fast I am traveling while my speedometer is reading 35?" The cop agreed. So I turned the car around and drove right up the road—and never came back! NOW who do you suppose was standing there scratching his head??

 **The Excuses**

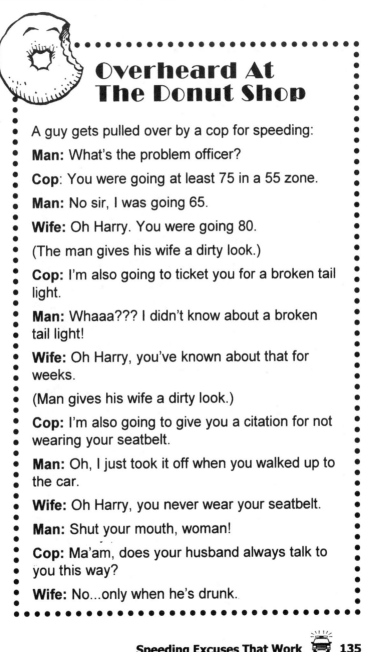

Overheard At The Donut Shop

A guy gets pulled over by a cop for speeding:

Man: What's the problem officer?

Cop: You were going at least 75 in a 55 zone.

Man: No sir, I was going 65.

Wife: Oh Harry. You were going 80.

(The man gives his wife a dirty look.)

Cop: I'm also going to ticket you for a broken tail light.

Man: Whaaa??? I didn't know about a broken tail light!

Wife: Oh Harry, you've known about that for weeks.

(Man gives his wife a dirty look.)

Cop: I'm also going to give you a citation for not wearing your seatbelt.

Man: Oh, I just took it off when you walked up to the car.

Wife: Oh Harry, you never wear your seatbelt.

Man: Shut your mouth, woman!

Cop: Ma'am, does your husband always talk to you this way?

Wife: No...only when he's drunk.

Subject: **Sweaty Disguise**
Date: Wed, 1 May
From: Σχοττ A<νφαππρ@ηομε.com >
To: copouts@copouts.com

I was traveling in Teaneck, NJ on a residential street doing 35 mph in a 55. Much to my dismay, a cop was waiting there with a radar gun. As I passed him, I looked him right in the eye. Then I pulled over before he could even turn his lights on, almost as if to say "You got me." He pulled up and asked, "Do you know why I pulled you over?" I admitted my guilt. While he check my documents, I noticed he kept looking at my chest area. As I peered down, I remembered I was wearing an NYPD sweatshirt I'd bought in a Manhattan souvenir shop. He asked "if I was on the job?" I answered yes, knowing he was asking whether I was a cop. If he asked for details, I would tell him what I did for a living—real estate appraising. On the other hand, if he *didn't* ask for details, I knew he would probably let me go out of professional courtesy. Then he handed back my paperwork and said, "all right brother, take it easy." I replied, "Thanks for the courtesy" and drove away ticketless. Who would have thought a $20 sweatshirt and a little "playing dumb" would save me so much aggravation?

Subject: **Saved By The Sun**
Date: Mon, 7 May
From: ϑορψ Σ<Ζιπϕορψ@ηομε.com >
To: copouts@copouts.com

I once got a ticket for illegal window tinting. In Kansas, the legal limit is 20% and I had 35% all the way around. When I went to court, I told the judge that I have Lupus, which is a sun-sensitive disease. I even brought a Lupus brochure and pointed that out. He read the pamphlet and dismissed the ticket.

Overheard At The Donut Shop

A police officer stopped a motorist for speeding down Main Street.

"But officer," the man began, "I can explain."

"Just be quiet," snapped the officer. "I'm going to let you cool your heels in jail until the chief gets back."

"But, officer, I just wanted to say…"

"And I say—keep quiet! You're going to jail!"

A few hours later, the officer looked in on his prisoner. "Lucky for you the chief's at his daughter's wedding. He'll be in a good mood when he gets back."

"Don't count on it," answered the fellow from his cell. "I'm the groom."

Subject: **Eyes Have It**
Date: Thurs, 31 May
From: Παυλ Λ <πλεωισ@μσν.com >
To: copouts@copouts.com

I was in the passing lane of a 4-lane highway, going 14 mph over the speed limit when a cop taking radar on the median pulled out and followed me for about 1/2 mile. He pulled me over and gave me a ticket. Because I had too many points already, this ticket would have cost me my license.

I entered the courtroom on the appropriate date— nervous because I did not have an excuse and thought I would lose my license for sure.

When my case was called, the trooper took the stand and explained in technical terms that he had captured me on radar and the gun had been tuned that morning with a tuning fork, and blah, blah, blah. He said he clocked me at 68 in a 55 on radar. I was screwed.

I asked the judge if I could ask the trooper a few questions, and this is basically how it went:

Me: How are you sure the car that went through your radar trap was mine?

Trooper: I saw you go past, I checked the radar, and I followed you.

Me: But how can you be 100% certain it was my car?

Trooper: I never took my eyes off your vehicle. I was able to glance at the radar screen without ever losing site of your vehicle.

Me: Are you certain you pulled over the same car you clocked? Is it *possible* you took your eyes off my car for just a moment and when you looked back up, you focused on a car other than the one that went through the radar trap?

Trooper: Like I said, I never took my eyes off of your vehicle. I watched you speed by and without ever taking my eyes off your car, I glanced down to read the radar screen. I could see you were going 68 mph without ever taking my eyes off your car, not even for a second.

Me: (Now I went for the kill...) You mean to tell me that you pulled right out into the fastlane of a busy highway without ever looking to see if someone was coming?

Trooper: Oh, well I guess I looked back quickly to make sure the traffic was clear.

Me: *Ah ha!* So you DID take your eyes off my vehicle!

Judge: Okay. Case dismissed.

Subject: **Beavis &...**
Date: Thurs, 17 May
From: ϑΧαρτερ <ϑχαρτερ@ηομε.com >
To: copouts@copouts.com

I was on patrol in eastern Oklahoma one afternoon when I clocked a guy in a pickup doing 80 mph in a 55 zone. I pulled him over, approached the driver and asked if there was an emergency or some other reason he was speeding.

He said he guessed he was just trying to keep his ears warm. I must have looked puzzled, because he then explained he must have had his head up his butt.

I just walked away laughing, got in my patrol car and drove away.

Subject: **Wheezer**
Date: Sat, 19 May
From: ϑΧαρτερ <ϑχαρτερ@ηομε.com >
To: copouts@copouts.com

I have asthma, so I always make sure I've left an empty inhaler in my glovebox. If I get pulled over, I start wheezing while trying to explain to the police officer that the reason I was speeding is because I've got to get to the drugstore to get a refill.

Overheard At The Donut Shop

A truck driver was driving along on the freeway, when he sees a sign that reads "low bridge ahead." Before he can react, the bridge is right ahead of him and he ends up getting stuck under the bridge. Cars get backed up for miles.

Finally, a police car shows up. The cop gets out and walks up to the truck driver, puts his hands on his hips and snickers, "Got stuck, huh?"

The truck driver, mustering all the sarcasm he can, replies, "No sir. I was delivering this bridge and I ran out of gas."

Subject: **High-Octane Gas**
Date: Thurs, 26 July
From: Σφισηερ <φισηερ333@αολ.com >
To: copouts@copouts.com

I was riding in my "modified car." By modified I mean that I stuck a device under the driver's side door that sprays out a horrid smelling gas (kinda like skunk meets rotten eggs). It sprays it out when you hit the button that's right near the automatic window buttons on the driver's side. This is an awesome gag at drive thru windows and that sort of thing. Well, I got pulled over one time and thought I'd give it a try.

The cop approached the door and asked for license and registration and I gave them to him. While he glanced them over, I pushed the button. Within 5-10 seconds, there was the most horrid smelling stench ever—he musta thought a skunk just sprayed him. Needless to say, he exclaimed, "Oh God, what the HELL is that smell?" and very shortly after said, "Well, you know what? I'm just gonna tear this up." Pinching his nose, he instructed us to take our records and roll up the window. I couldn't believe it!!! I was *soooo* amazed that my "fart machine" worked.

Subject: **Let Us Spray**
Date: Sat, 21 July
From: ϑαχκP<ϑαχκρ@αoλ.com >
To: copouts@copouts.com

I was in a little B-210
station wagon doing
71 mph in a 50 on a
rural farm road in
Denton, Texas.
There was no
other traffic on
the road. My wife
was busy fixing her hair, and the windows were rolled
up. Out of the corner of my eye, I saw the cop clock
me with his radar as I crowned a low hill. I quickly
swerved and decelerated. As he came up behind me, I
slowed to a stop and pulled over, rubbing my eye.

I asked him what the problem was and he told me
about the 71 in a 50. I proclaimed that my wife was
doing her hair and had accidentally sprayed her
hairspray in my eye. I guess I'd rubbed it so hard, the
cop said it was really red, and I'd better rinse it out
with water. He let me go, saying there was a
convenience mart three miles up the road.

To avoid a New York traffic jam, I ignored a 'NO LEFT TURN FROM 7 TO 9:30 AM EXCEPT SCHOOL BUSES' signs, even though it was 9:15. As soon as I turned, there was a cop pulling drivers over, including 5 other illegal left-turners before me. Having time to think before he reached my car, I was struck by a great idea. I advanced my watch 20 minutes.

"Do you know why I pulled you over?" he snapped.

"Yep," I said. "Because I'm an idiot."

He looked straight at me. *"Excuse me?"*

Then I laid it on. "To keep myself from running late, last night I started putting my watch ahead 20 minutes. Today, I forgot all about it, and I thought I was making a legal turn." So I showed him my watch, which indeed confirmed my story. He laughed, shook his head, and handed me back my license. This was AFTER he had given tickets to the other five. "Happy birthday!" he said.

Subject: **Diamond Lane**
Date: Thurs, 12 July
From: ΒιλλΒιλλ <ΒιλλΒιλλ@ηομε.com >
To: copouts@copouts.com

My late friend Mike was doing 85 mph in a posted 65 zone. He was pulled over by a Mass state police officer who asked him what the rush was. Noting it was a female cop, as well as Christmas Eve, he produced the engagement ring he'd just purchased for his girlfriend.

"My girlfriend says I'm afraid of commitment and she's getting on a plane to Florida in ONE hour," he improvised. "If I don't propose to her before she goes, I know I'll never see her again. This is either going to be the best or worse Christmas of my life. It's all up to how long it takes you to write me the citation. I'd appreciate it if you'd hurry ma'am." She gave him a verbal warning to take it slow, and Mike was on his way.

Subject: **Urine Trouble**

Date: Wed, 23 May

From: Κελλψ T<Κελλψ T23@αολ.com >

To: copouts@copouts.com

My brother's friend keeps a water bottle in the car with him at all times. If he gets pulled over, he pours the water into his lap and tells the cop he's got bladder problems. He's gotten out of three tickets now.

> **Editor's Note:** Don't forget to stash the water bottle.

Subject: **What's Shakin'?**
Date: Thurs, 26 April
From: σταχψ <Σταχψ387@ηομε.com >
To: copouts@copouts.com

A buddy and I were speeding along and got pulled over. Before the cop came up to the car, I told my buddy to act like he was epileptic, and spill a little pop on his crotch. When the cop came up to the window, my friend was having seizures and drooling. The wet spot on his pants added nicely to the effect.

When the officer asked why I was speeding, I told him it was because my friend has epilepsy and I was afraid he was going to swallow his tongue.

At that moment, the seizures stopped and I promised to get him home to get his medication.

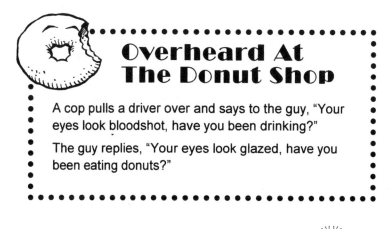

Overheard At The Donut Shop

A cop pulls a driver over and says to the guy, "Your eyes look bloodshot, have you been drinking?"

The guy replies, "Your eyes look glazed, have you been eating donuts?"

Subject: **Flashing Headlights**
Date: Thur, 29 Mar
From: Αχεχο<αχεχο@γτε.net >
To: copouts@copouts.com

Even my friends don't believe me, but I swear this actually happened to me. I was heading home on the 110 Freeway one Friday afternoon. Next thing I know, I look over and see this red convertible Mustang passing me on the left. Then I couldn't believe it—this really cute blonde in the passenger seat just lifts off her top and winks at me. I almost lost it!!!! They're laughing and getting all crazy as they start pulling away. I tried to keep up, but they took off into the carpool lane, which goes up higher for a few exits. I couldn't follow them, but I never took my eyes off them either, which is probably why I didn't see the cop right behind me until he yelled at me over his loudspeaker to pull over.

So I pull over and this cop tells me he's been following me at 80 mph for at least a couple of miles. So I say, "Dude, you gotta understand! This babe riding in a Mustang just flashed me the two most unbelievable…" I stopped. I didn't know how to say it to the cop. So then I said, "And she winked at me, too!! Then they bailed into the carpool lane. I was just trying to keep up with them because she was SO HOT!"

I musta looked really bummed, because after he checked my license and registration, he said, "Okay, 'dude'—you've had enough misery for one day. But don't let me catch you speeding again."

P.S. I found out later that some local radio show has something called a Flash Friday and those girls were probably flashing everyone.

Subject: **Lead Foot**
Date: Thur, 17 May
From: Αχεχο<αχεχο@γτε.net >
To: copouts@copouts.com

When I get pulled over for speeding, I just tell the officer I was on my way to the hospital to have surgery. When the cop asks what for, I just say, "I'm going to have the lead taken out of my foot!"

It always gets a good laugh from the officer, and I've never gotten a ticket yet.

Overheard At The Donut Shop

One night a police officer was staking out a rowdy bar for DUIs. After last call, he watched a guy stumble out of the bar, trip on a curb, and try five different keys before finally getting into his car. Then the guy fumbled around with his keys for several more minutes. Meanwhile, everyone else left the bar and drove off. Finally, the guy started his engine and began driving away. The officer pulled him right over, read him his rights, and gave him a breathalyzer test. The results were 0.0. Puzzled, the officer demanded to know how that could possibly be. "Easy!" replied the driver, "I'm the designated decoy."

Subject: **Beat The Pizza**
Date: Thur, 6 Sept
From: Αχε<αχεχο33@αολ.net >
To: copouts@copouts.com

It was one of those 12-hour days on the job. I had to skip lunch because we were all behind schedule and my boss was breathing down my neck. By the time 6 o'clock rolled around, I was freakin' starving. So just as I'm leaving, I phoned the local pizza delivery place and ordered the Works.

So I'm rushing home to beat the pizza guy and of course some cop comes out of nowhere. "What's the hurry?" he wants to know. So I tell him: "I'm trying to beat my pizza home." He says, "Whaaa?" I say, "Sorry man, it's been a 12-hour day with no lunch. I ordered the Works just as I left the job and I got to get home quick before the delivery guy gets there." I musta looked pretty damn hungry, because he let me go with a warning.

P.S. It's a good thing he let me go—I beat the pizza guy by 2 minutes!

Subject: **Speechless**
Date: Thurs, 31 May
From: Αχιε <αχιε86@μσν.com >
To: copouts@copouts.com

Unfortunately, a botched operation on my vocal cords left me unable to speak. As a result, I carry a pad of paper with me everywhere I go, which really sucks because my handwriting's terrible. But there is one thing my situation is good for: speeding tickets. I've been pulled over twice since my operation, and I've started greeting the officer with a great big "HELLO," written on my pad of paper. It's funny, they always seem to be speechless, too. Not one of them has ever had the heart to write me a ticket. I guess they feel pretty sorry for me.

Once I had a buddy in the car with me who witnessed this whole thing. He was so inspired, he decided to try it himself the next time he was stopped. What do you know—it worked!

> ***Editor's Note:*** *Stash the cell phone before trying this one.*

Subject: **Wannabe Cop**

Date: Thurs, 26 April

From: Αχεψ<αχεψ55@εαρτηλινκ.net >

To: copouts@copouts.com

Even though I'm young, I've managed to escape a number of tickets using a simple little gimmick.

When I get pulled over, I'm always very respectful and cooperative when I happen to mention that I'm studying to go into law enforcement. I keep several "textbooks" in the car at all times…usually in the backseat in plain view. They include a couple of criminal law books, a copy of the latest Vehicle Code, and a Police Report Writing book. I always say something like, "I hope this ticket won't hurt my chances of making the force." I guess their "professional courtesy" extends to wannabe cops as well, because I haven't gotten a ticket yet!

> ***Editor's Note:*** If you use this one, be sure to do a little "research" on the school you're "attending" in case he asks questions.

Subject: **Speed Pass**
Date: Fri, 20 July
From: ☐Ρογερ Δοδγερ <Δοδγερμ@ηομε.com>
To: copouts@copouts.com

I work for a local police department as a dispatcher in New Jersey, so I know a few of the ways that work—and don't work—for getting out of speeding tickets.

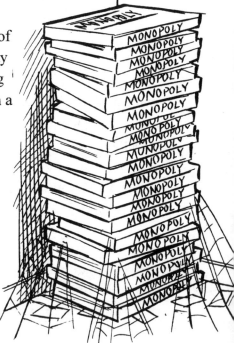

Once on the night shift, one of the officers told me that a guy he'd pulled over for speeding in a 25 mph area handed him a card he figured was a laminated PBA card.. But guess what? It turned out to be a laminated 'Get Out Of Jail Free' card from a Monopoly game board! He said it cracked him up, as he'd never gotten that excuse in 18 years on the job—so he let the guy go.

Resource Guide

Beat The Cops—The Guide To Fighting Your Traffic Ticket And Winning by Alex Carroll. Okay, so what happens if your excuse doesn't fly? Get my other book! It's fun, easy to read, and it works.

National Motorists Association ... This is the motorists' rights organization that among many notable accomplishments, got the 55 mph speed limit repealed. Not only that, but they will actually pay your speeding ticket fine! Really. Call them to join: 800-SPEED-TRAP. Tell 'em I sent you. Or visit *www.motorists.org.*

SpeedTrap.com ... This great resource for all motorists includes a vast list of speed traps worldwide.

Casey Raskob, Esq. ... This excellent attorney specializes in New York State traffic law. A great guy, too. Reach him at *www.speedlaw.net* or (914) 271-5383.

SpeedLabs.com ... Carl Fors knows more about speed measurement and detection devices than anyone else on the planet.

A Speeder's Guide To Avoiding Tickets ... by Sergeant James Eagan (Avon). This is a *great* book. Highly recommended. Jim's been a friend for many years. And get this: this former cop is now a traffic court judge!

Beat Your Ticket ... by David Brown, JD, (Nolo). If you really want to understand all the legal stuff, you'll appreciate this detailed book.

Beating The Radar Rap ... by John Tomerlin. This book really gets into the technical details of how radar works ... and doesn't work. Good information.

How To Talk Your Way Out Of A Traffic Ticket ... by David Kelley. A very inexpensive, insightful, chatty little book by this longtime CHP officer.

There are lots of other books out there, and I've leafed through most of them. But since I haven't actually read them ... I can't honestly rate them. I will say that the ones I've read are the ones that caught my eye.

Ever seen
a celebrity...

...get a ticket?

You're our eyes and ears for real-life ticket stories and traffic stops involving movie stars, musicians, sports heroes, politicians, big wigs and famous CEOs.

And if you're a cop whose stopped or ticketed a celebrity—here's your chance to unload!

Just e-mail *copouts@copouts.com* with your celebrity stories—the juicier the better!

P.S. If you're a celebrity (or a president), we'd love to hear from you, too.

Are YOU A Weasel?

Now it can earn you fabulous prizes!

Did you ever weasel your way out of a ticket? Then look what you now can win...

★ A FREE PASS on your next speeding ticket (we'll pay it for you!)

★ A FREE Radar Detector—the latest top-of-the-line model

★ A 1-year subscription to your favorite car magazine

★ A life-sized plush toy weasel—for you or your sweetheart

★ Plus more prizes, including an autographed copy of *Speeding Excuses That Work.*

How To Enter

Visit **copouts.com** and tell us your wildest, wickedest Weasel-out-of-a-ticket story. If yours is selected for a Weasel Award, you're eligible for these prizes and more!

Come to **copouts.com** now. We give away prizes each week!

Complete rules and official entry form only at **copouts.com**. Prizes subject to change without notice. Void where prohibited.